Global/International Issues and Problems

Other Titles in This Series

Economics: A Resource Book for Secondary Schools, James E. Davis and Regina McCormick

Geography: A Resource Book for Secondary Schools, A. David Hill and Regina McCormick

U.S. Government: A Resource Book for Secondary Schools, Mary Jane Turner and Sara Lake

U.S. History, Volume 1—1450-1865: A Resource Book for Secondary Schools, James R. Giese and Laurel R. Singleton

U.S. History, Volume 2—1865 to the Present: A Resource Book for Secondary Schools, James R. Giese and Laurel R. Singleton

Global/International Issues and Problems

A Resource Book for Secondary Schools

Lynn S. Parisi and Robert D. LaRue, Jr.

Social Studies Resources for
Secondary School Librarians, Teachers, and Students
James E. Davis, Series Editor

ABC-CLIO

Santa Barbara, California
Oxford, England

Library of Congress Cataloging-in-Publication Data

Parisi, Lynn.
    Global/international issues and problems : a resource book for
secondary schools / Lynn S. Parisi, Robert D. LaRue, Jr.
       p. cm. — (Social studies resources for secondary school
librarians, teachers, and students)
    Bibliography: p.
    Includes index.
    1. World politics—1945- —Study and teaching (Secondary)
I. LaRue, Robert D. II. Title. III. Series.
    D843.P364   1989   909.82—dc19   89-30325

ISBN 0-87436-536-8 (alk. paper)

96 95 94 93 92 91 90 89   10 9 8 7 6 5 4 3 2 1

ABC-CLIO, Inc.
130 Cremona, P.O. Box 1911
Santa Barbara, California 93116-1911

Clio Press Ltd.
55 St. Thomas' Street
Oxford, OX1 1JG, England

This book is Smyth-sewn and printed on acid-free paper ∞ .
Manufactured in the United States of America

Contents

Figures

Introduction: How To Use This Reference Work

This resource book has been written for the secondary librarian, social studies teacher, and student. The narrative information is presented in a nontechnical manner and is intended to provide helpful introductory information for the study of international issues and global perspectives. Although not exhaustive, the resources cited encompass the majority of useful current materials available for teaching and learning international studies at the secondary school level. Because this volume provides annotated bibliographic information regarding reference and classroom materials that can assist teachers in selecting course content and can be used for class assignments or special projects, this work can serve as a supplementary text for use within the classroom as well as a research resource. The following is a description of how each section of this work might be used.

Chapter 1, "Defining a Global Education by Its Content," provides an effective framework for global education within the curriculum. In this chapter, reprinted with permission from *Social Education,* Willard M. Kniep of Global Perspectives in Education emphasizes the content as the organizer of the discipline. For the teacher who is designing a new course or wishing to infuse a global perspective into a variety of existing courses, this chapter will be helpful in selecting course content and strategies.

Chronologies of milestone events in international affairs comprise Chapter 2. This chapter contains a separate timeline for each of the content strands of global education identified in Chapter 1. The events highlighted are selective and are designed to provide the user with a context and a starting point for exploring international relations and developing global perspectives.

"Biographies of Contemporary Global Figures," Chapter 3, is arranged in alphabetical order by last name. Each biography provides an introduction to a contemporary figure who has played a pivotal role in international affairs, whether from a political, economic, environmental, or technological perspective. The biographies highlight the impact each figure has had on the development of international relations.

Chapter 4, "World Data," presents both quantitative data (charts, graphs, and maps) and source material (international treaties and agreements). In many cases, the statistical data have been simplified from the original source material for easier understanding. The user is encouraged to go beyond the charts and graphs presented in this chapter for more detailed and comprehensive statistics. The purpose of the data included in this chapter is to give students or teachers a sense of significant economic, social, political, and technological conditions around the world, as well as to provide an introductory statistical vehicle for exploring global connections and trends. Source material—charters and agreements—included in this section are also designed as introductory material. They are included as examples of landmark agreements and relationships among the nations of the world.

Many organizations and groups provide information, resources, and services in global education and international studies. Chapter 5, "Directory of Organizations, Associations, and Government Agencies," describes these organizations. Arranged alphabetically by name, both public and private groups and organizations are included, as well as government agencies. Also cited are organizations whose specific function is to promote and coordinate educational travel and exchange programs for secondary students and/or educators. Students and teachers can use the directory to find the following information concerning each group: address, telephone number, name of president or contact person, descriptions of the purpose of the organization, and its publications and periodicals.

Chapter 6, "Reference Works," is an annotated bibliography of reference materials that can be used by both students and/or teachers as they conduct research and participate in classroom and library projects. Complete bibliographic information and costs, in addition to brief descriptions, are provided with each entry. (ISBNs are also provided whenever possible.) The reference materials are organized according to format or type. Following the first section, which cites general reference works, the reference materials are arranged alphabetically by title, except as noted. They include:

General Reference Works. This section provides descriptions of general reference works. References include a datacard file and an index to newspaper editorials that students can use to conduct research in international studies.

Annual Editions. Many annual publications contain information of interest to students and teachers of global issues. Included in this section are collections of readings on international topics and additional reference works.

Atlases. Atlases are an excellent source of world data and global comparisons. Many of the atlases cited here develop specific themes within global and international studies, such as world revolutions, the Third World, and so on. Both students and teachers will find the maps and the discussions provided in the atlases cited very useful.

Bibliographies. This section contains bibliographies of resources for social studies teachers interested in infusing a global perspective into their courses as well as those teaching specific units on international studies. Included are guides describing print materials, audiovisuals, and computer software.

Encyclopedias. Encyclopedias with specific relevance to international relations and issues are cited in this section. These publications can be excellent sources of information for general overviews and special research projects. Many of those cited focus on specific themes within the realm of global and international studies.

Handbooks. This section includes surveys, statistical summaries, and information digests useful to both students and teachers as they do research and classroom assignments.

Online Databases. In the section dealing with online databases we offer resources for an ideal situation in which schools have an unlimited supply of money and computers and are teaching students to use computers to access information. Such a situation is increasingly common across the United States. The many online databases that students can use to obtain information on historical and contemporary international events are described. The databases cited are available through one or more of the following services:

> BRS Information Technologies
> 1200 Route 7
> Latham, NY 12110
> (800) 468-0908

> CompuServe
> 5000 Arlington Center Boulevard
> P.O. Box 20212
> Columbus, OH 43220
> (800) 848-8199

Dialog Information Services, Inc.
3460 Hillview Avenue
Palo Alto, CA 94304
(800) 3-DIALOG

Dow Jones News/Retrieval
P.O. Box 300
Princeton, NJ 08540
(609) 452-1511

For each database, we include computer connect-hour costs (this does not include telecommunications costs, usually around $9 per connect-hour using UNINET, TELENET, or TYMNET), and citation costs. Citation costs given are for the full record. Citation costs for BRS, which has various pricing options, are for maximum citation charges. Other citation costs are for educational rates, as noted.

Periodicals. The listing of periodicals is a very selective one. Cited are those periodicals specifically concerned with global education and international relations. Not included are specialized academic periodicals or periodicals from other countries. For information concerning additional journals and newsletters, students and teachers should refer to the "Directory of Organizations, Associations, and Government Agencies" in Chapter 5.

Printed Indexes. The indexes described in this section can be used by both students and teachers to locate information for research projects and assignments. Both general indexes and subject-specific indexes are easy to use, and students will need only a brief introduction by the school librarian or media specialist; the use of other indexes will require more instruction. By using the indexes, students and teachers can access a vast array of pertinent information through journal articles, statistics sources, biographies, dissertations, research reports, classroom materials, and news digests.

Teacher Resource Materials (arranged by author). This section describes additional resources for teachers, including teaching models, background readings, curriculum guides, rationales for global education, and reports on the status of global education in the United States.

Chapter 7 contains annotated listings of classroom materials. Complete bibliographic information, grade levels, and prices, as well as a brief description, are provided for each item. Entries are organized under sections alphabetically arranged by type of material. Sections include:

Computer Software. This section describes microcomputer software programs in global and international education. This instructional tool provides a new teaching method for illustrating ideas and topics in today's increasingly interdependent world. The types of software programs are indicated in the listing for each entry. These are (1) drill and practice (stimulus-response format); (2) tutorials (lessons conducted essentially in the form of a dialogue, i.e., the program presents lesson material and then asks questions to determine whether the student understands the material); (3) simulations and games (programs that model events, problems, or other phenomena); and (4) databases (collections of information and statistics). The systems on which the software programs can be used are also indicated in the listing.

Note: The software market is constantly changing as new programs are produced and old programs are revised or become obsolete. Substantial time and effort was taken to make this section as complete and as thorough as possible; however, there are likely to be some unintended errors and omissions.

Multimedia Kits. There are many very good multimedia programs dealing with international affairs and issues. Included in this section are slide and filmstrip programs as well as kits containing audio and visual materials and transparencies. These descriptions should help teachers choose those best suited to their needs.

Simulations and Games. Another excellent way to supplement an international studies course is through the use of games and simulations. A great variety are described in this section. For example, students can simulate companies and businesses engaged in international trade, role-play diplomats, develop hypothetical countries, and so on.

Supplementary Print Materials (arranged by author). This section is must reading for teachers looking for materials to supplement their courses. Included are fiction, nonfiction, student activities, lesson plans, puzzles, essays, mini-units, photographs, cartoons, and case studies.

Textbooks (arranged by author). Teachers looking for new global studies textbooks to use in the classroom will find the overviews of the texts provided in this section very helpful. Texts generally fall into three categories: world history using a global approach, world geography using a global approach, and texts specifically designed for a global studies program.

Videocassettes and Films. Teachers looking for videocassettes or films to supplement their international and global lessons will find this section of interest. These two media are excellent ways to enliven a classroom and stimulate discussion. Videocassette formats are indicated.

The "Glossary of Terms" provides definitions of terms selected to include the ideas and concepts most common to global and international learning in economics, politics, technology, and human rights.

An index has been provided to further enhance the reader's use of this work. Teachers and students can consult the index for specific subjects or items of particular interest. This section may also be used as a source of potential research topics or project ideas. The table of contents and index provide readers with easy access to that information in this volume most pertinent to their needs.

HOW TO ORDER ERIC DOCUMENTS

Some sections of this work cite ERIC documents. These are identified by an ED (ERIC Document) number. All ERIC documents can be ordered from the following address:

ERIC Document Reproduction Service (EDRS)
3900 Wheeler Avenue
Alexandria, VA 22304-5110
(800) 227-3742

These documents are also available in microfiche in libraries throughout the country that subscribe to the ERIC system. Check the library nearest you.

Defining a Global Education by Its Content

by Willard M. Kniep

THE GLOBAL EDUCATION MOVEMENT has generated an impressive body of literature over the past two decades.[1] A good deal of it demonstrates the need for global education—both in terms of the changing world in which we live and the lack of knowledge among U.S. students about their world. Many of these publications set out the goals of global education and describe how those goals can be infused into the existing school curriculum.[2] And an increasing number of teaching materials are available to help teachers offer instruction on specific topics, concepts and issues associated with global education.

However, substantive descriptions of the content that should be included in a K–12 curriculum incorporating a well-thought-out scope and sequence seem lacking. What aspects of present and past global realities ought to be included in the curriculum of elementary and secondary schools if they are to offer an education that is truly global? What content should teachers be teaching and what information should students be learning in an education for a global perspective? These important questions about the substance of a global education have been largely unaddressed in the global education literature.[3]

The consequence of this omission is that we are asking policy-makers to buy a "pig in a poke" when we urge them to adopt programs for which we have no substantive descriptions. Global education programs are likely to be widely adopted and implemented only when this situation is remedied. Until we have developed substantive descriptions of the content of a global education, we will lack a full, helpful and convincing answer for the skeptics and uninitiated who ask: "What is global education?"

Reprinted from *Social Education* (Vol. 50, No. 6, October 1986, pp. 437–446) with permission of the National Council for the Social Studies. Willard M. Kniep is vice president for research and development, Global Perspectives in Education. For a more complete discussion of this topic, see *Next Steps in Global Education: A Handbook for Curriculum Development,* New York: Global Perspectives in Education, 1988.

It is, after all, its content that distinguishes global from other kinds of education. Many of its goals—critical thinking, valuing diversity, seeing connections—can also rightly be claimed by other disciplines and movements in education. So too, the processes and methods that we promote as part of a global education. What is unique about global education is its substantive focus, drawn from a world increasingly characterized by pluralism, interdependence and change.

What follows, then, is an attempt to provide a framework for thinking about the content of a global education. It is not meant to be the definitive answer for what specific bits of information students should learn, nor is it intended to suggest how that content is to be organized and taught. Rather, it is meant to stimulate thought and dialogue about our common ground, the essential and basic substance of an education that is worthy of the name "global."

The process of developing this framework has been an exercise in integrative thinking. The four organizing elements were developed from an analysis of curriculum materials and theoretical and descriptive literature in global education. For the descriptions of the specific elements, I have drawn heavily on the writing of a number of experts from the fields represented within those elements. The references at the end of the article include the work I have leaned upon most heavily.

The content of a global education is drawn from the present and historical realities that describe and define the world as a global society. In order to bring some order to thinking about those realities and to organize the content, I propose four elements of study as being essential and basic to a global education: the study of human values, the study of global systems, the study of global problems and issues, and the study of the history of contacts and interdependence among peoples, cultures and nations. Unless these four elements are included, educational programs will fall short of being truly global.

STUDYING HUMAN VALUES

The values that people hold reflect their attitudes and beliefs and are shaped by their experiences. Our values determine how we view the world, and they influence our decisions and behaviors as we undertake life's activities. While some of our values are personal and idiosyncratic—like tastes and preferences—many of the most important are shared within our ethnic, national and religious groups.

Other values are shared so broadly, transcending our other identities, that they may be thought of as universal and as defining, in part, what it means to be human.[4] In a global education, we are concerned primarily with the universal human values that transcend group identity and the diverse values that define group membership and contribute to our unique perspectives and worldviews.

Universal Values

In the 20th century, for the first time, the world's people—in all their diversity of religious, philosophical and ideological beliefs—have begun to draft universal standards for human relations. This effort has taken place largely under the auspices of the United Nations. It has resulted in a nearly universal acceptance by the nations of the world of a common position for what it means to be human.

Human rights have historically been thought of as legal guarantees derived from being a citizen of a particular nation. A major shift in the last half of this century has been to the idea that we have certain rights because we are human beings. In 1948 the United Nations produced the Universal Declaration of Human Rights asserting that all human beings are entitled to life, liberty, property, equality, justice, freedom of religion, free speech, peaceful assembly and asylum. It outlawed slavery, torture and arbitrary imprisonment or detention. The Declaration, in addition to these civil and political rights, addressed human social and economic rights: the right of everyone to a standard of living that will assure health and well-being; to adequate food, water and shelter; and to security in sickness and old age.

These universal values have their origins in a variety of cultural, religious and national traditions. As different as these traditions are, they have espoused many of the same values regardless of time and geography. In today's world, the language of these values is seen in the foundational documents of many of the world's nations. Certainly, these values were a major force in the founding of the United States and are firmly embedded in the Declaration of Independence and the Constitution.

To offer these values as universal does not imply that they are universally accepted and implemented. In fact, the struggle to achieve the standards for human life and interaction that they imply has been an evolutionary process. The effort is very new. Participation in the effort is still limited. The task of codifying global standards for what it means to be human is hardly a task to be achieved in only a few decades.

If our students are ultimately to find their place in this global process, they must see their relationship as U.S. citizens with the task of evolving and defining standards for human relations by learning about the struggles of humankind to implement those standards. Our job is to help students relate those struggles to their own cultural and national values.

Diverse Human Values

In a global education, we must also provide students with the opportunity to engage with and understand the diversity of the world's peoples. The cultural differences that go with group membership are the most obvious manifestation of the variety of values and perspectives among human beings. These differences are reflected in people's tastes, preferences, attitudes, lifestyles and worldviews. They are the product of a people's unique evolutionary adaptation to their environment and circumstances in order to fill a set of needs common to all groups.

A global education helps students to see commonality within this diversity. All peoples have developed a material culture—housing, foods, dress, tools, possessions, etc.—that fit their needs and environment. They have developed unique forms of aesthetic expression, work and play, language and other systems of communication. They have evolved social organization and the means for social control, formal and informal systems for education and transmission of social values, traditions and rituals for expressing their worldview and beliefs, and mechanisms and organizations for carrying out various economic functions.

Ultimately, we must help our students to perceive the qualities of humanness that they share with those different from themselves. They need to see that there are a variety of values in the world, some different from their own, that are rooted in tradition, and that have the legitimacy of experience and history for those who hold them.[5] In the bargain, they will gain a measure of self-understanding by experiencing commonality in human differences and by seeing themselves through the eyes of those with another worldview.

STUDYING GLOBAL SYSTEMS

We experience linkages with people throughout the world to an extent unprecedented in history. This interdependence is the result of our participation in a world in which systems predominate. While not a new phenomenon, the magnitude and scope of interdependence—and our awareness of it—has been greatly increased since World War II. The change can be traced to advances in science and technology that have seemed to shrink our world and also to changes in interaction among states that have come with the creation of the United Nations and the breaking up of traditional colonial empires.

Because we live simultaneously in a number of interacting global systems, we experience a cumulative sense of global interdependence. All of these systems have certain common characteristics: each has a set of component parts or actors that interact within the system according to some procedures or mechanisms which either help or inhibit the system's functioning. To truly understand these systems we must know their components, possibilities for interaction, and rules for contact and influence.

A focus on the interdependent nature of our world lies at the very core of programs in global education. In order to help students understand the pervasive nature of that interdependence, our programs must engage them in the study of the global *economic, political, ecological* and *technological* systems in which they live.[6] Ultimately, students will be enabled to participate effectively and responsibly in their world to the extent to which they see their place as actors within these systems and to the degree to which they have acquired the knowledge, skills and motivation necessary for effective and responsible participation in them.

Economic Systems

For most of us, our economic behaviors provide the most striking and obvious examples of our individual interdependence with the rest of the world. It is easy to trace not only how we depend on other areas to supply many of the goods that we consume daily, but also how producers in other parts of the world depend on our demand for the goods they are producing.

The global economy is a highly complex system producing interdependencies far beyond a cause and effect relationship between one consumer and one producer in two different parts of the world. The study of this system should help students unravel some of this complexity by focusing their attention on the actors, their motivations and how they make decisions. Moreover, their study should engage them in tracing relationships among actors in order to see their place in the web of interactions.

The global economic system is primarily a capitalistic, market economy in which the source of economic activity is the profit motive. Decisions about what is produced and for whom it is produced are determined both by the marketplace and by political forces. Households, multinational firms and states export products in which they have a comparative advantage—products that they can produce more cheaply than foreign competitors or alternatives produced at home. The same economic forces lead these actors to import from others products not so cheaply or so well produced at home.

Political factors influence production as states participate in and support international financial institutions like the World Bank and the International Monetary Fund. Political factors also influence the degree to which a state's economy is involved in world trade and finance by encouraging free trade and an open economy or by imposing tariffs and other protectionist devices that tend to limit participation in the international economy.

Interactions within the system are characterized by a broad range of activities. Multinational assemblage of goods, ranging from chocolate bars to automobiles, is common. So too are foreign investment by multinational corporations, international lending, and the buying and selling of foreign currencies.

Because of the complex web of linkages, actions by any of the actors usually have consequences for other actors within the system. While these consequences are sometimes predictable, often they are unexpected, unintended and even unknown. The closing of plants in one part of the world may be instrumental in creating new jobs in another part of the world. Increases or decreases in interest rates charged by banks in the United States due to the effects of a federal budget deficit affect the amount that nations with large debts will have to make in annual payments to those same banks. This in turn determines how much money will be available within that country to provide its citizens with basic human needs. And the ability or inability of farmers on one continent to produce an annual crop has far-reaching effects not only for the availability of food on that continent but also on the prices that farmers in other parts of the world receive for their crops. The price that consumers around the world will pay for their food is a direct outgrowth of this chain of effects.

A global education will help students see themselves as actors within this global economy. Because they all participate in the economic system, as consumers, producers and citizens, many opportunities are available for students to trace linkages from themselves to other actors. By providing these opportunities, we enable students to see how they are affected by other actors within the system and how their own decisions and lifestyles affect many people around the globe.

Global Political Systems

Current world events demonstrate dramatically the interdependence of political activity around the world. An election in the Philippines, and the subsequent change in that nation's power structure, is watched intently around the world because of its implications for the security of Asia and for the balance of power among the world's superpowers. United States fiscal policy, commonly viewed as a domestic matter, affects many other national economies and, ultimately, the ability of some governments to sustain broad popular support among their citizens and to stay in power.

The priorities and policies set by the politburo of a communist nation for its next five-year plan—for industrialization, agriculture or the introduction of the profit motive into the economy—affect the lives of millions of North American farmers, workers, stockholders and travelers. The extension or denial of human rights to citizens in one Central American country has implications for the influx of refugees into neighboring countries and may even result in a debate within the U.S. Congress about our immigration policies. The list of examples goes on. Each day's events provide their own proof of the linkages among the actors who make up the global political system.

This system, dominated by sovereign nation-states, is a means for exerting influence and power and, perhaps even more than domestic political systems, is influenced by economic concerns related to distribution of the earth's resources. Yet, it is not a system of government that holds authority over all of the world's people. It has only a limited body of laws and no formal mechanisms of coercion and enforcement. Even the United Nations must rely solely on the collective power of its members to deter aggression and to bring the nations in the international system into closer cooperation and mutual reliance to attack common problems such as poverty, disease and illiteracy.

Since it lacks a mechanism for coercion and enforcement, the international political system operates through bargaining and negotiation based on national self-interest, coercive military and economic power of individual states and alliances, and the power of world opinion and status. Within this framework, a relatively small core group of the powerful nations are dominant, deriving their power from military, economic, technological and ideological strength.

While nation-states are among the most noticeable and dominant actors in the global political arena, they are by no means the only ones. Opportunities for participation in world affairs have escalated dramatically since World War II. This era has seen the emergence of more than

20 semi-autonomous international organizations that are part of the UN system and a proliferation of regional organizations whose member nations share economic or security interests.

Presently more than 4,200 international nongovernmental organizations work to influence national and international policies on a wide range of global issues, thus playing a role in world politics similar to that of pressure groups in domestic politics. Decisions made in all of these organizations are important to more and more of the world's people as they struggle to solve their problems.

Subnational governments—e.g., cities and states—are also becoming increasingly active in international trade, cultural exchanges and even in foreign policy issues like apartheid and a freeze on nuclear weapons.

The cast of characters increasingly includes businesses, the media and special interest groups. The role of transnational corporations in international affairs is growing. Electronic media, particularly U.S. television networks, have become not only observers and reporters of international events but also actors in shaping or resolving those events. Even terrorist groups have become an increasingly important force.

In the United States, as in many other democratic countries, individuals play an important role in the global system to the extent that they exercise their rights of participation. Because of the dominant role of the U.S. as the world's leading democratic power, the effects of our actions as individual citizens on others are extraordinarily clear and strong. Because of this privileged position, and the responsibilities that go with it, we have an extraordinary need to be informed about our world and to see our linkages to the rest of the world. Our students have the same needs if they are to participate effectively and responsibly as U.S. citizens in the global political system.

Ecological Systems

The planet on which we live is a sphere of rock orbiting around the sun and bathed in radiant energy and the solar wind. Beneath its crust, it is white hot and molten. Upon its surface, continents float and ocean floors spread. Between its dynamic surface and the vacuum of space above is the thin, fragile layer composed of humans, plants, animals, and microorganisms that are interdependent with one another and that depend upon land, oceans, and elements to sustain life.

Within the earth's complex ecological system, the biosphere, the thin blanket of life that surrounds the globe, is readily affected and easily threatened by human activities.[7] The earth's biosphere is a living system that is continuously rebuilding the biochemical bases of life and thereby permitting life-support structures and food chains to exist and flourish. Life is found at elevations as high as 10,000 meters in some mountain ranges and as deep as 10,000 meters in some parts of the ocean.

However, the zone of primary biological reproduction is an extremely thin layer ranging from approximately 100 meters in the tallest forests to only a few meters deep in most bodies of water. The thinness of the biosphere in relation to the earth is akin to the layer of morning dew on the surface of an apple. The earth's green cover is a prerequisite for the rest of life. Within this life realm, every organism is linked, however tenuously, to every other as all living things are caught up in the cycling of energy and nutrients from sun, water, air and earth.

Of all the species that make up life on the planet, human beings, because of our capacity to manage and exploit, maintain or destroy, have become the most critical actors in the ecological system. A global education will emphasize for our students the interdependent and symbiotic relationship of living and nonliving things and the special role that we human beings play in the ecological system. Above all, a global education will help them to feel part of the living world, to respect it and their unique place in it, and to undertake individual actions only after consideration of their actions on the whole ecological system.

Technological Systems

There is little question that we live in the age of technology. While technology has always played an important role in the lives of human beings and for the systems in which they live, the technologies of our age—based on jet engines and rocketry, transistors and microchips, nuclear fission and fusion—are changing life on our planet to an extent and with a rapidity unimagined in previous generations. Not only are modern technologies transforming the way individuals live, work and relate to one another and to their environment; their influence is dramatically changing geopolitics, the functioning of the world economy and the global ecological system.

Much of the interconnectedness of people and nations characterizing the modern world is due to the rapid technological advances in transportation and communication—the two primary means of human contact. These advances have served both to shrink our world in terms of the time that it takes to cover distances and to enlarge our world in terms of the sheer number of people, places, events and bits of information that are available to us.

The unprecedented ability to transport people and goods throughout the world has fundamentally changed the world economy. The ability to move weapons across great distances through unmanned rocketry has changed basic conceptions of warfare and has profoundly affected the balance of power and the nature of diplomacy within the global political system. The capacity to provide instantaneous coverage of events around the globe through satellite communication has not only made the whole world more accessible to more people but has also changed the role of media. Moreover, global radio and television networks, by their ability to inundate one culture with the ideas, values, and products of another, have the potential for undermining and changing a culture's basic ideas and values.

One of the most interesting side effects of modern technology has been the transformation of information into a dominant resource. The convergence of computer and telecommunications technologies has vastly increased not only the amount of information to which people have access, but also their ability to organize and use that information. Furthermore these technologies provide a whole range of new possibilities for the future in how we relate to other people, employ increased leisure time, use our minds, and carry out new vocations and occupations.[8]

Certainly, a global education will provide students with the opportunity to explore these possibilities and to experience and tinker with the latest technology. Ultimately, the study of technological systems will enable students to understand the rapid transformation of the world toward a global society, to explore the ramifications of that transformation on the world's people and cultures, and to develop knowledge and skills for living in and coping with an increasingly complex world.

STUDYING GLOBAL ISSUES AND PROBLEMS

For all of us, part of reality consists of being bombarded daily by international problems and issues. If young people are to be well informed about their world, their education must engage them in inquiry about the causes, effects and potential solutions to the global issues of our time. As in the study of systems, students must see how they affect and are affected by these problems and issues. Ultimately, they deserve to see how they may be part of global issues and problems and how they may contribute to their resolution or solution.

What are the characteristics of global issues and problems? First, they are *transnational* in scope. The origins and consequences of the problem go beyond the borders of any single nation. Second, they will be solved only through *multilateral actions:* solutions or resolutions cannot be achieved by the actions of only one state.

This reality leads to the third characteristic of a global issue: a degree of *conflict* is inherent in each. This conflict is rooted in disagreement about the nature and cause of the problem, in differing values and goals related to outcomes and means, and in the difficulty of finding appropriate actions necessary for securing a desirable outcome. Fourth, these problems and issues are characterized by *persistence.* They have evolved as problems and issues over time and they are likely to persist in some form into the future. Finally, they are *linked* to one another. Solutions to one problem generally will have an effect on some factors related to the other problems.[9]

For thinking about the content of a global education, I have developed four general categories into which the majority of global issues and problems seem to fall. Each corresponds to a movement to infuse education about that issue into the curriculum: peace education, development education, environmental education and human rights education.

Peace and Security Issues

The contemporary world in which we live is one in which national security is nearly a global obsession. Each year the countries of the world spend an estimated $750 billion, 6 percent of the global GNP, to arm themselves. This amounts to almost $150 for each person on the earth. Since World War II, although not a single war has been legally declared, at least 160 armed conflicts have occurred in which an estimated 16 million people have lost their lives.[10] Overlaying all of these events is the constant threat of nuclear war, which raises the possibility of eliminating life as we know it on this planet.

Fundamentally, nations see their security in terms of the presence or absence of threat to any of their basic values or to the basic resources upon which they depend for their livelihood and well-being.[11] Concerns for security are diverse, ranging from the protection of human rights and national autonomy to maintaining economic and food independence.[12] Achieving security and maintaining peace have been preoccupations of nations throughout history because the international system lacks a central authority to enforce laws and resolve conflicts with a system of sovereign nations.

A number of basic questions must focus the inquiry of students about international peace and security issues: What is security? What alternatives to armed conflict and the threat of mutual destruction are available to provide security? What influences the security policy of states and how do these policies relate to other problems, such as development issues and environmental concerns? How do individual citizens influence the security policies of their nations?

Development Issues

The study of development issues will engage students in the struggles of peoples and nations to meet their basic needs, achieve national economic growth, and expand their political, economic and social independence. This study will focus primarily on the cluster of issues and problems surrounding the widening gap between the rich and the poor peoples of the world and the inequality and suffering that this gap represents.

We can grasp the dimensions of this gap between rich and poor by comparing the richest fifth of the world's population—some 1.1 billion people, including almost everyone in the United States—to the poorest fifth. Statistics for 1980 show that per capita annual income for the richest fifth was $9,470; for the poorest fifth it was only $206, a ratio of 46 to 1. Other comparisons for the two populations are just as revealing: adult literacy was 97 percent vs. 42 percent; government health expenditures per capita were $432 to $2 and educational expenditures were $497 to $6; average life expectancy was 74 years vs. 53 years; and the percentages of each population with access to safe water were 96 and 39 percent respectively.[13]

This gap between rich and poor—and the attendant hunger, disease and injustice—can hardly be ignored. It is a threat to global security and to the environment. It is a major cause of Third World financial indebtedness, which is so extensive and intractable that it threatens to bring down the international banking system. And for many people, in a world of ample resources it is morally and psychologically intolerable.

The study of development issues begins with the basic question of what is development and underdevelopment. It will involve students in coming to grips with a broad range of the world's current problems: overpopulation, hunger, famine, desertification, deforestation and other forms of environmental degradation, North-South and East-West relations, appropriate technology and technology transfer, the Third World debt crisis and many other problems and crises that fill our daily headlines. The key is for students to discover how they relate to the problems of development and the consequences of underdevelopment and, more important, how they can become involved in the search for solutions to these pressing problems.

Environmental Issues

Environmental issues are primarily those concerned with the consequences of human exploitation and management of the earth: its lands, oceans and elements. Problems associated with the consequences of human activity on the environment are not new, but, because of a rapidly expanding human population and a worldwide increase in consumerism, those consequences have been magnified, in some cases, into problems of crisis or near-crisis proportions. Acid rain, pollution of streams and oceans, atmospheric build-up of carbon dioxide, industrial emissions into the air we breathe, endangered species of wild plants and animals, depletion of rain forests and overgrazing of the world's grasslands are just a few of them.

These problems, and the issues attendant on solving them, are important to all human beings, because we all share the same earth, and to the thousands of different kinds of plants and animals with which we also share the planet. All of them transcend national borders and require solutions that involve a variety of actors. A global education will enable students to see their role in relation to these issues and problems as well as the role of the other actors and systems to them. The major focus of their study will be on considering and analyzing solutions and on the need for collaborative, multilateral actions in finding those solutions.[14]

Human Rights Issues

The decades since World War II have been a time of unmatched interest in and concern for human rights throughout the world. To a great extent, this condition is an outgrowth of humanity's horror and outrage over the persecution and genocide of millions of Jews and other innocent civilians before and during the war. The United Nations Declaration of Human Rights is a direct result of that reaction.[15]

A second reason for the unprecedented contemporary concern for human rights flows from the unprecedented interconnectedness of the modern world. Not only do people have greater awareness of human rights issues through the global communications networks, but more people can experience a greater sense of membership in the world community and identify personally with those who suffer from a denial of human rights.

Despite the Declaration and other efforts of international bodies, we still live in a world where large numbers of people are denied basic human rights. Genocide, apartheid, political repression and imprisonment, persecution of indigenous peoples, censorship, religious persecution, torture and denial of homelands daily make up headlines and stories in broadcast media. A global education would be incomplete if it did not come to grips with this paradox: the global community embraces in principle the concept of universal human rights while there is still widespread denial and abuse of those rights.

Grounded in the history and values of their own country, our students must be given the opportunity to study how other nations and peoples of the world conceive of human rights. They must, if racism and oversimplification are to be avoided, see human rights and their abuses around the world in historical and cultural contexts. As civic actors, consumers and producers, and part of the most powerful and influential nation in the world, U.S. citizens play an important role in the global arena of human rights. Students must see their part in this arena as they take political decisions and actions, as they support and participate in churches, unions, corporations and private voluntary organizations, and as they make choices in the economic marketplace.

What can be done to assure that the rights we enjoy can also be enjoyed by our fellow human beings around the world? What can I or my government do to help others acquire basic human rights? How do we deal with the tensions and contradictions between differing world-views—e.g., individual rights vs. the well-being of the group; self-determination vs. fatalism; equal rights for all vs. culturally determined status based on sex or caste—that inevitably arise in the debate over human rights? How do we avoid ethnocentrism and cultural imperialism in our concern for human rights on the one hand and moral and cultural relativism on the other? Students in a global education will have the opportunity to grapple with such questions and issues in their own development as U.S. citizens and as members of a fragile world community.

STUDYING GLOBAL HISTORY

A historical perspective, including a grasp of the evolution of universal and diverse human values, the historical development of our contemporary global systems, and the antecedent conditions and causes of today's global issues and problems is fundamental to a global education.[16]

Unfortunately, the histories studied by most of our students do little to develop that kind of perspective about today's interdependent world.

So-called "world histories" are often primarily histories of Western civilization or of the spread of Western influence to the rest of the world. Often they are the histories of separate regions with little attention to relations among them. Usually these histories focus on the development of the states that are the most powerful in the contemporary world.

In general, traditional approaches to the study of world history add little to the understanding of contemporary worldwide interdependence because they do not emphasize the historical roots of that interdependence. Yet if our students are to truly understand the contemporary interdependence of the world, they must be grounded in the knowledge that contact and exchange among civilizations has been more or less continuous for the last 2,000 years.

The beginnings of these connections—which the historian William McNeill refers to as "the ecumene"—are evident in the contact of civilizations that stretched from Spain and North Africa to the China Sea during the time of the Roman and Han Empires.[17] Links were by sea, by land routes through the Middle East, and by the movement of nomads. Disease passed with ease among civilizations. Migrations of useful plants and animals occurred. Cotton, sugar cane and chickens, domesticated in India, spread to China and Eurasia. Technological secrets moved more slowly. Indian steel was exported to the Roman Empire, but the technology for making it was not. Chinese silk was exported to India, the Middle East and Rome from the 2nd century A.D. but the secret of its manufacture did not reach the outer world until the 6th century.

Yet for most U.S. students, world history begins with the exploits of the great European explorers. By including the concept of the ecumene we can help our students place their discoveries in a new light. People had explored and exploited the whole world and shared their advances for centuries before the emergence of the Europeans. The French historian Fernand Braudel asserts that even the inventory of vegetable resources had been drawn up so precisely since the beginning of written history that not one single nutritious plant of general usefulness was added by the European explorers to the list of those previously known.[18]

Other historians believe, based on concrete similarities between Asian and American cultures, that there were influences from Asia on developing societies in the Americas. To support their theories, they point out that a thousand years before Columbus, ships were crossing from Ceylon to Java with 200 passengers, that by the time of Augustus, ships of 75 tons were crossing the Indian Ocean, and that the Chinese had ships of up to 800 tons by 700 A.D.

Contact, exchange and interdependence have continued throughout history. The global ecumene, which was created by the European explorers of the 15th and 16th centuries, has been accelerated through the continuing contacts of migration, trade and warfare of the past 400 years and has been transformed in today's world by global air travel and satellite communication.

A grasp of this concept provides our students with an indispensable perspective for understanding present world relations in their historical context. This is particularly true for understanding present relations between the United States and the Third World and between the United States and the Soviet Union. To build such a perspective, we need to provide our students with a broad historic panorama that includes conditions, contacts, colonization and dependencies that are the antecedents of today's international relationships.

The framework I have presented here is meant to stimulate thought and dialogue about what we want our students to know as the basis for developing a global perspective. If others disagree with the specific elements I have chosen to organize the framework, I hope that they will be motivated to develop alternative descriptions of the substantive basis for a global education. For if we are serious about integrating a global perspective into the teaching of the broad range of subjects and across the spectrum of age levels, then we must develop substantive descriptions to serve as maps for those concerned with program development and implementation.

The most useful function of this framework, or others that are developed, is as a tool to assess the adequacy of existing programs and as a guide to develop new programs and curricula for a global education. We may expect to find the substantive elements in a variety of places across the curriculum.

Obviously, all of the elements are an essential part of instruction in history, geography, and the other social sciences. But literature, music and the arts have a great deal to contribute to the understanding of human values, the experience of people around the globe in coping with the persistent problems and issues of our time and to the development of a historical perspective.

Not only is the study of systems fundamental to the physical, natural and biological sciences, but the application of scientific knowledge is also directed toward solutions of persistent problems. While the social studies may have a special role to play in the development of a global perspective, school programs will be truly global when the distinctive content of a global education is reflected across the curriculum.

NOTES

This essay was prepared at Global Perspectives in Education as part of a project supported by grants from the Exxon Education Foundation, Ford Foundation and Rockefeller Foundation. The opinions and recommendations expressed are those of the author and do not necessarily reflect the views of the funders or Global Perspectives in Education.

[1]See Kniep (1985) for a review of the literature of global education since 1967.

[2]One of the most eloquent and durable statements of the goals of global education is found in Hanvey (1978). See also Becker (1979) for a thorough treatment of both goals and strategies for programs in global education.

[3]One reason for the lack of substantive definitions of global education may be that some of its most influential writers have taken a philosophical position against them. Anderson (1979), for example, contended that global education "is not a domain of education that can be defined in terms of content, subject matter, or discipline," but rather is a movement with certain grassroots aspects that are needed to ensure that it is responsive to changing world realities and to the unique needs and contexts of students in local schools and communities.

[4]Alger and Harf (1984) make this assertion as part of their rationale for a global education.

[5]The NCSS's (1979) own statement on the role of values in the social studies presents and extends this point of view. I believe that we must engage our common sense when teaching about diverse values if we are to avoid the pitfalls of cultural and moral relativism. Obviously some value positions (e.g., the superiority of one race over another or government by a ruling elite) do not stand up very well to comparative scrutiny using as a standard the basic values (e.g., human dignity, justice, democratic participation) that we as a society espouse. The implication is that our students must be well grounded in the history and values of their own cultures and nation.

[6]The categories within this scheme are based to a large extent on Kenneth Boulding's (1985) description of the systems in which we live. In order to develop a workable framework for looking at the substance of curriculum, I have combined his physical and biological systems into my description of the ecological system and included aspects of his social system within economic and political systems. My technological system is substituted for his communication system. Some of the points in his evaluative system are included in the previous section describing the study of human values.

[7]I recommend *GAIA Atlas* (1984) as an eloquent description of our planet as a living organism.

⁸Information as a resource has been a recurring theme of Harlan Cleveland's (1985) writing.

⁹These characteristics are an adaptation and extension of Alger and Harf's (1984) description of global issues.

¹⁰For current statistical descriptions and national breakdowns of expenditures on arms, I recommend Sivard's (1985) booklet which is published annually, and many of the charts assembled by World Eagle (1985).

¹¹For an extension of this definition see McGowan and Woyach (1988).

¹²See Cleveland's perceptions of the real threats to global security in this issue.

¹³Taken from McGowan and Woyach (1988). For more extensive data and analysis I recommend Sewell, et al. (1985) and the annual updates by the World Bank (1985).

¹⁴See the special issue of *Social Education,* Blackburn (March 1985), for a more extensive description and rationale for engaging students in the study of environmental issues.

¹⁵I have relied heavily for this description on the work of Gruber and others in the special September 1985 issue of *Social Education* focused on human rights.

¹⁶Both Anderson (1979) and Alger and Harf (1984) have placed heavy emphasis on the historical perspective in their rationales for global education.

¹⁷*Ecumene,* from the French, has the same root as "ecumenical." McNeill (1963) characterizes the ecumene as the process of civilizations coming into regular contact and resulting in extensive cultural borrowing.

¹⁸See Braudel (1981).

REFERENCES

Alger, Chadwick F., and James E. Harf. *Global Education: Why? For Whom? About What?* Columbus, OH: Ohio State University, 1984.

Anderson, Lee. *Schooling for Citizenship in a Global Age: An Exploration of the Meaning and Significance of Global Education.* Bloomington, IN: Social Studies Development Center, Indiana University, 1979.

Becker, James, ed. *Schooling for a Global Age.* New York: McGraw-Hill, 1979.

Blackburn, Anne M., guest ed. "Currents in Environmental Studies." *Social Education* 49 (March 1985): 198–218.

Boulding, Kenneth E. *The World As a Total System.* Beverly Hills, CA: Sage Publications, 1985.

Braudel, Fernand. *The Structures of Everyday Life: Civilization and Capitalism, 15th–18th Century,* Vol. 1. English Translation. New York: Harper and Row, 1981.

Cleveland, Harlan. "Educating for the Information Society." *Change* (July/August 1985): 13–21.

Hanvey, Robert G. *An Attainable Global Perspective.* New York: Center for Global Perspectives, 1978.

International Bank for Reconstruction and Development/The World Bank. *The Development Data Book.* Washington, DC: The World Bank, 1985.

Kniep, Willard M. *A Critical Review of the Short History of Global Education: Preparing for New Opportunities.* New York: Global Perspectives in Education, 1985.

McGowan, Patrick, and Robert B. Woyach. "An International Relations Approach to the Tenth Grade World Studies Course." In *Approaches to High School World Studies,* edited by Richard C. Remy and Robert B. Woyach. Boston: Allyn and Bacon, 1988.

McNeill, William. *The Rise of the West: A History of the Human Community.* Chicago: University of Chicago Press, 1963.

Myers, Norman, ed. *GAIA: An Atlas of Planet Management.* Garden City, NY: Anchor Press/Doubleday and Co., 1984.

National Council for the Social Studies. "Revision of the NCSS Social Studies Curriculum Guidelines." *Social Education* 43 (April 1979): 261–278.

Sewall, John W., Richard E. Feinberg and Valeriana Kallab, eds. *U.S. Foreign Policy and the Third World: Agenda 1985-1986.* New Brunswick, NJ: Transaction Books, 1985.

Sivard, Ruth Leger. *World Military and Social Expenditures, 1985.* Washington, DC: World Priorities, 1985.

Totten, Samuel, guest ed. "International Human Rights Education." *Social Education* 49 (September 1985): 444–538.

World Eagle. "World Military Expenditures." *Worldview Posters.* Wellesley, MA: World Eagle, 1985.

Chronology of Events of Global Importance, 1945-1987

2

GLOBAL POLITICAL SYSTEMS

Date	Event
1945	Yalta Conference.
	United Nations Charter signed.
	League of Nations holds final meeting.
	V-E Day ends war in Europe, May 7.
	Germany divided into four zones of occupation.
	Spain excluded from UN.
	Three-power occupation of Berlin begins.
	Potsdam Conference.
	Japan surrenders August 14: end of World War II.
	Vietnam formed as independent nation.
	Arab League founded to oppose creation of Israel.
	Nuremberg trials of Nazi war criminals begin.
1946	UN General Assembly holds first session in London.
	New York is declared permanent UN headquarters.
	Albania, Hungary, Transjordan, Bulgaria become independent states.
	Churchill gives his "Iron Curtain" speech, Fulton, Missouri.
	East German Social Democrats merge with Communists.
	Referendum makes Italy a republic.
	Paris Peace Conference.
	Nuremberg verdict: 12 sentenced to death.
	Power in Japan transferred from emperor to elected assembly.
1947	United States withdraws as mediator in Chinese civil war.
	Peace treaties signed in Paris.
	Burma proclaimed independent republic.
1948	Communist coup d'etat in Czechoslovakia.
	Hague Conference for European Unity.
	Israel comes into existence as a state.
	Soviet Union blockades Berlin; airlift begins.
	British Citizenship Act grants citizenship to all Commonwealth citizens.

Date	Event
1949	People's Republic of China proclaimed.
	North Atlantic Treaty signed.
	Republic of Eire proclaimed.
	Berlin blockade lifted.
	German Federal Republic proclaimed.
	Apartheid system established in South Africa.
	East Germany established as democratic republic.
	India adopts constitution as federal republic.
	Holland transfers sovereignty to Indonesia.
	France transfers sovereignty to Vietnam.
1950	West Germany joins Council of Europe.
	North Korean forces invade South Korea.
1951	Peace treaty with Japan signed in San Francisco.
1952	Honolulu Conference of three-power Pacific Council (United States, Australia, New Zealand).
	Israel and Germany agree on restitution for damages by Nazis.
1953	Korean armistice signed at Panmunjom, July 27.
1954	Soviets reject idea of a reunited Germany.
	Dien Bien Phu taken by Vietnamese Communists.
1955	Soviet Union decrees end of war with Germany.
	Vienna Treaty restores Austrian independence.
1956	Sudan proclaimed independent democratic republic.
	Pakistan becomes Islamic republic.
	Soviet Union enters Hungary and ignores UN censure.
	Japan admitted to United Nations.
1957	Franco announces that the Spanish monarchy will be restored on his death.
1958	Egypt and Sudan join to form the United Arab Republic.
	Alaska becomes forty-ninth state of United States.
1959	Fidel Castro becomes premier of Cuba.
	Cyprus becomes a republic.

Date	Event
1960	United States admits to spying on Soviet Union with U-2 planes when one is shot down.
	Summit talks among Khrushchev, Macmillan, Eisenhower, and de Gaulle; they fail.
	Belgian Congo granted full independence.
1961	Bay of Pigs invasion by United States fails.
	Berlin Wall constructed.
1962	Cuban missile crisis.
	Uganda and Tanganyika become independent.
1963	United Arab Republic, Syria, and Iraq agree to union.
	Buddhist coup overthrows government of Vietnam.
	Kenya becomes independent republic within Commonwealth.
1964	Zanzibar declared republic; unites with Tanganyika to form Tanzania.
	Moise Tshombe declares Congo a people's republic.
	Nyasaland becomes independent Malawi within Commonwealth.
	Malta becomes independent within Commonwealth.
	Kenya becomes republic.
	Arafat takes over leadership of Al Fatah.
1965	Gambia becomes independent.
	Rhodesia declares independence.
	Gambia, Singapore, Maldives join United Nations.
1966	British Guiana becomes independent nation of Guyana.
1967	Six Day War is fought in Middle East.
	King Constantine and family flee military coup in Greece.
1968	Mauritius independent within Commonwealth.
1969	Arafat becomes chairman of Palestine Liberation Organization.
	Anguilla breaks all ties with Britain.
	United States agrees to return Ryukyu Islands to Japan.
1970	Gambia proclaimed republic within Commonwealth.

Date	Event
1971	China admitted to United Nations.
1972	United States returns Okinawa to Japan.
	Ceylon becomes Republic of Sri Lanka.
	Martial law declared in Philippines.
1973	U.S.–South Vietnam/North Vietnam–Vietcong sign cease-fire agreement.
	Bahamas granted independence.
1974	Bloodless coup begins democratic reform in Portugal.
	United States and East Germany open formal diplomatic relations.
	Portuguese Guinea granted independence as Guinea-Bissau.
	Grenada declares independence.
1975	Communist forces overrun South Vietnam.
	Sikkim becomes an Indian state.
	Northern Marianas residents vote to become U.S. citizens.
	Leaders of 35 nations sign Helsinki Accord.
	People's Democratic Republic of Laos proclaimed.
	Angola, Mozambique, Cape Verde, Sao Tome and Principe, Papua New Guinea, and Surinam become independent.
1976	North and South Vietnam reunited.
	Seychelles Islands declare independence.
	Republic of Transkei proclaimed.
1977	Palestine National Council calls for an independent nation.
	Afars and Issas become Republic of Djibouti.
	United States and Panama sign new Panama Canal Treaty.
	Bophuthatswana declared independent.
1978	United States and People's Republic of China establish full diplomatic relations.
	Solomon Islands and Tuvalu become independent nations.
1979	Egypt and Israel sign peace treaty.
	Iranian revolution forces Shah to leave Iran.

Date	Event
1979 *(cont.)*	Panama takes possession of Canal Zone.
1980	Strikes in Poland set up free trade unions.
	Rhodesia becomes nation of Zimbabwe.
	New Hebrides becomes independent Vanuatu.
1981	UN votes not to readmit South Africa.
	Anwar Sadat assassinated by Moslem extremists.
1982	Rising worldwide concern over nuclear weapons.
1984	Britain and China sign treaty on future of Hong Kong.
	United States withdraws from UNESCO.
1985	U.S.-Soviet arms talks continue.
	United States refuses to acknowledge World Court ruling against U.S. actions in Nicaragua.
1986	Soviet Union enters period of "restructuring" and "openness."
1987	United States and Soviet Union reach tentative agreement on intermediate-range nuclear missile treaty.

GLOBAL ECONOMIC SYSTEMS

Date	Event
1945	World War II ends.
1946	United Nations meets for first time.
1947	George Marshall proposes European Recovery Program (Marshall Plan).
1948	U.S. Congress passes Marshall Plan. Price of uranium rises to $1,600 per ton.
1949	United States grants $5.43 billion to Europe. Britain devalues pound sterling.
1950	Rapid growth in production and sales of consumer goods begins in United States.
1951	Arab League begins economic blockade of Israel, initiating a permanent state of war.
1952	Industrial, agricultural, and social institutions forcibly collectivized in People's Republic of China.
1953	London Conference of Commonwealth prime ministers.
1954	France and West Germany sign cultural and economic pact.
1957	"The Six" sign Rome Treaty: beginning of the Common Market.
1958	European Common Market created. Britain and Spain sign trade pact.
1959	European Free Trade Association ratifies treaty.
1960	Gross national product of the United States reaches $502.6 billion; decade-long economic boom in the capitalist world begins.
1961	Latin-American Free Trade Association established.
1962	Anglo-French agreement reached on joint construction of the Concorde supersonic aircraft.
1963	Britain rejected for Common Market membership.
1964	British "brain drain" as scientists leave for United States. Britain grants licenses to drill for oil in North Sea.
1969	Nobel Prize for Economic Science awarded to Ragnar Frisch and Jan Tinbergen for their development of econometrics.
1972	Petroleum shortage first becomes apparent.

Date	Event
1973	Arab oil embargo to United States, Western Europe, and Japan in retaliation for their support of Israel; causes worldwide energy crisis.
1974	Worldwide inflation causes dramatic increases in costs of fuel, food, and materials; oil-producing nations boost prices, worsening inflation; economic growth slows to near zero in most industrialized nations.
	Nobel Prize for Economics awarded to Gunnar Myrdal and Friedrich A. von Hayek.
1975	Egypt reopens Suez Canal.
	Nobel Prize for Economics awarded to Leonid V. Kantorovich and Tjalling C. Koopmans.
1976	Nobel Prize for Economics awarded to Milton Friedman.
1977	Nobel Prize for Economics awarded to Bertil Ohlin and James E. Meade.
1978	Nobel Prize for Economics awarded to Herbert A. Simon.
1979–1985	Worldwide, economies suffer due to high energy prices, global tensions, and slow recoveries.

GLOBAL TECHNOLOGICAL SYSTEMS

Date	Event
1945	First atomic bomb detonated near Alamogordo, New Mexico, July 16.
1946	Electronic brain built at University of Pennsylvania.
1947	U.S. airplane first flies at supersonic speeds. Transistor invented.
1948	200-inch Mount Palomar reflecting telescope dedicated.
1949	Soviet Union tests its first atomic bomb. United States launches first guided missile.
1950	Einstein's general field theory of relativity published, elaborating his 1905 special theory of relativity.
1951	Electric power produced from atomic energy.
1952	Contraceptive pill produced. First hydrogen bomb exploded.
1953	Soviet Union explodes hydrogen bomb.
1954	Dr. Jonas Salk starts inoculating children with polio serum.
1956	Transatlantic telephone service starts. Oral vaccine for polio developed by Albert Sabin.
1957	Soviet Union launches Sputnik I and II, first earth satellites.
1959	Soviet Union launches rocket with two monkeys aboard.
1960	U.S. scientists develop first laser. United States launches first weather satellite.
1961	Yuri Gagarin (USSR) is first man to orbit the earth. Alan Shepard makes first U.S. spaceflight.
1965	First flight around the world over both poles.
1968	Second decade of the World Health Organization celebrated.
1969	Apollo 11 lands on lunar surface.
1970	747 jumbo jet begins regular flights.
1971	Human growth hormone somatropin successfully synthesized.
1972	Space travel becoming a commonplace in American minds.

Date	Event
1974	India becomes sixth nation to explode nuclear device.
1975	United States and Soviet Union link space vehicles.
1976	Discovery of viral cause of multiple sclerosis.
1977	Space shuttle Enterprise makes first manned flight.
	United States confirms testing neutron bomb.
1978	First test-tube baby born.
1979	Accident at Three-Mile Island nuclear plant, which threatened meltdown, traced to design error.
1982	Heart transplants becoming more common.
	Compact disc technology perfected for music and computer data storage.
	Dr. Barney Clark becomes first recipient of a permanent artificial heart.
1983	Human immune deficiency virus, cause of AIDS, isolated.
1984	Bruce McCandless and Robert Stewart become first humans to fly untethered from a spacecraft.
1986	25th U.S. space shuttle launch, of shuttlecraft Challenger, ends in explosion.
	Major nuclear accident at Chernobyl, USSR, kills 23 and forces evacuation of 40,000.
1987	Global fight against AIDS begins.
	Development of high-temperature superconducting compounds.
	U.S. Commerce Department issues patents on life forms created by gene splicing.

GLOBAL PEACE AND SECURITY ISSUES

Date	Event
1945	Yalta Conference.
	United Nations Charter signed.
	End of war in Europe, May 7.
	Potsdam Conference.
	First atomic weapons used at Hiroshima and Nagasaki.
	Arab League founded to oppose creation of Israel.
1946	UN General Assembly holds first session in London.
	Churchill gives his "Iron Curtain" speech, Fulton, Missouri.
	Paris Peace Conference.
1947	European Recovery Program (Marshall Plan) proposed.
	United States withdraws as mediator in Chinese civil war.
	Peace treaties signed in Paris.
	Cominform established at Warsaw conference.
1948	Marshall Plan approved by U.S. Congress.
	Hague Congress for European Unity.
	Soviet Union blockades Berlin; airlift begins.
1949	North Atlantic Treaty signed.
	People's Republic of China declared.
	Statute of Council of Europe established.
	Berlin blockade lifted.
1950	Soviet Union and People's Republic of China sign 30-year pact.
	North Korea invades South Korea.
	United States signs military assistance pact with France, Cambodia, and Laos.
1951	Peace treaty with Japan signed in San Francisco.
1952	European Defence Community Treaty signed in Paris.
	Honolulu Conference of three-power Pacific Council (United States, Australia, New Zealand).
	China and Mongolia sign ten-year agreement.
1953	London Conference of Northern and Southern Rhodesia and Nyasaland.
	London Conference of Commonwealth prime ministers.
	Korean armistice signed at Panmunjom, July 27.
	United States and Korea sign mutual defense treaty.

Date	Event
1954	British, French, U.S., and USSR foreign ministers meet in Berlin; Soviets reject idea of German reunification.
	U.S.-Japanese defense agreement.
	U.S.-Britain Potomac Charter signed.
	Southeast Asia Treaty Organization (SEATO) established.
	United States and Canada agree to build distant early warning radar system.
	Burma and Japan sign treaty.
	United States signs pact with Nationalist China.
1955	Soviet Union decrees end of war with Germany.
	Italy, West Germany, and France establish European Union.
	West Germany becomes NATO member.
	Vienna Treaty restores Austria's independence.
1956	Soviet Union enters Hungary and ignores UN censure.
	Japan admitted to United Nations.
1957	United States and Israel issue Declaration of Washington.
1958	"Eisenhower Doctrine" formulated for protection of Middle East nations from Communist aggression.
	United States and Britain hold Bermuda Conference.
	International Atomic Energy Agency established.
	European Common Market created.
1960	Khrushchev, Macmillan, Eisenhower, and de Gaulle meet in Paris; summit talks fail.
1961	Kennedy and Khrushchev meet in Vienna to discuss disarmament, Laos, and Germany.
	Berlin Wall constructed.
1962	Cuban missile crisis.
1963	United States and Soviet Union agree on "hotline" communications system.
	Nuclear testing ban signed by United States, Soviet Union, and Great Britain.
1964	UN peace force takes over in Cyprus.
	Tonkin Gulf incident alleged.

Date	Event
1965	Ho Chi Minh rejects peace talks with United States.
1966	International Days of Protest (against U.S. policy in Vietnam).
1967	Soviet Union and Britain agree to help achieve peace in Vietnam.
	Egypt and Jordan sign mutual defense pact.
1968	Israel and United Arab Republic agree to prisoner exchange.
	Czechoslovakia invaded at night by Soviet Union.
1969	United States agrees to return Ryukyu Islands to Japan.
	First U.S. troops withdrawn from Vietnam.
1970	Israel and United Arab Republic agree to 90-day cease-fire.
	Soviet Union and West Germany sign friendship treaty.
	Paris peace talks end second full year with no progress toward peace in Vietnam.
1971	People's Republic of China and United States begin era of détente.
	People's Republic of China admitted to United Nations.
	United States and Soviet Union sign treaty banning nuclear tests on ocean floor.
1973	Ireland, Britain, and Denmark join European Economic Community.
	U.S.–South Vietnam/North Vietnam–Vietcong sign cease-fire agreement.
	Arab-Israeli war heats up again.
	East and West Germany establish diplomatic relations.
	United States and Soviet Union sign treaty to limit nuclear war.
1974	United States and East Germany establish formal diplomatic relations.
1975	United States ends two decades of military involvement in Vietnam.
	Leaders of 35 nations sign Helsinki Accord.
	Forty Islamic nations vote to expel Israel from United Nations.

Date	Event
1976	United States and Soviet Union sign treaty limiting size of underground nuclear tests.
1977	United States and Panama sign new Panama Canal treaties.
1978	United States and People's Republic of China announce establishment of full diplomatic relations.
	Soviet Union and Vietnam sign 25-year friendship treaty.
	Japan and People's Republic of China sign treaty of peace and friendship.
	Anwar Sadat and Menachem Begin agree on framework for bilateral peace treaty.
1979	Israel and Egypt sign peace treaty.
	Soviet Union invades Afghanistan.
1980	Rising world terrorism.
	Greece is reintegrated into military wing of NATO.
1981	Antinuclear arms movements gain strength throughout Europe and the United States.
	Egyptian President Anwar Sadat assassinated by Moslem extremists.
1982	Rising world concern over nuclear weapons.
	Israel invades Lebanon, forcing the Palestine Liberation Organization to agree to a peaceful withdrawal.
1983	Soviets shoot down unarmed South Korean commercial airliner when it strays into Soviet airspace.
1984	Indian Prime Minister Indira Gandhi assassinated by Sikh extremists.
1985	U.S.-Soviet arms talks.
	United States refuses to acknowledge World Court rulings against U.S. actions in Nicaragua.
1986	Soviet Union enters period of "openness" and "restructuring."
1987	United States and Soviet Union reach tentative agreement on intermediate-range nuclear missile treaty.

GLOBAL DEVELOPMENT, ENVIRONMENTAL, AND HUMAN RIGHTS ISSUES

Date	Event
1945	Black markets for food, clothing, and cigarettes develop in Europe.
	International Bank for Reconstruction and Development founded with authorized capital of $27 million.
	Women's suffrage permitted in France.
1946	Women ensured the vote in Italy.
	World population in millions: China, 455; India, 311; USSR, 194; U.S., 140; Japan, 73; West Germany, 48; Italy, 47; Britain, 46; Brazil, 45; France, 40.
	United States tests atomic bomb at Bikini.
1947	More than one million U.S. veterans enroll in college under G.I. Bill of Rights.
	Jackie Robinson becomes first black in major league baseball.
1948	U.S. Congress passes Marshall Plan.
	First World Health Assembly meets in Geneva.
	World Council of Churches organized.
1949	U.S. Foreign Assistance Bill grants $5.43 billion to Europe.
	Apartheid system established in South Africa.
1950	U.S. Library of Congress contains 8.6 million books.
	World population is 2.3 billion.
	City populations in millions: London, 8.3; New York, 7.8; Tokyo, 5.3; Moscow, 4.1.
	United Nations reports that of 800 million children, 480 million are undernourished.
	1.5 million television sets in United States.
1951	Industrial and commercial business workers as a percentage of all workers: Britain, 46; Germany, 41; U.S., 30; Italy, 29; Japan, 20; India, 10.
1952	West Germany becomes member of World Bank.
1954	France and West Germany sign cultural and economic agreement.
	United States publishes 1,768 newspapers; 59 million copies daily.
	United States contains 6% of world population; 60% of all cars; 58% of all telephones; 45% of all radios; 34% of all railroads.

Date	Event
1954 (cont.)	Concern rises over fallout and disposal of radioactive waste.
1957	Cities with over one million population number 71.
	Desegregation crises in Little Rock, Arkansas.
1959	World Refugee Year proclaimed.
1960	Television sets in millions: U.S., 85; Britain, 10.5; West Germany, 2; France 1.5.
1961	World population in millions: China, 660; India, 435; USSR, 209; U.S., 179; Japan, 95; Pakistan, 94; Brazil, 66; West Germany, 54; Britain, 53.
	Tanganyika conference to protect African wildlife.
1962	Total world population is 3.1 billion; 1.6 billion adults of which 44% are literate.
	Rachel Carson publishes *Silent Spring.*
1963	Major religions in millions of followers: Christians, 890; Hindus, 365; Buddhists, 200; Jews, 13.
1965	U.S. legislature supports national antipollution laws.
1966	West German autobahn system contains more than 2,000 miles.
	Supermarket concept spreads throughout Europe and Asia.
	U.S. vehicle registrations total 94 million.
	Color televisions become popular.
	International Union of Official Travel Organizations estimates that 126 million tourists travel the world.
1967	Cost of living rises worldwide: 1.8% in United States to 5.8% in New Zealand.
	Sweden changes from right-side to left-side driving.
1968	Columns of the Parthenon in Athens are in danger of collapsing as a result of weathering, acid rain, and foundation erosion.
	Television sets in millions: U.S., 78; USSR, 25; Japan, 20.5; Britain, 19; West Germany, 13.5; France, 10.
	Second decade of the World Health Organization celebrated.
	Aswan High Dam completed.

Date	Event
1969	Red Cross flies relief into a starving Biafra.
	Representatives of 39 nations meet in Rome to survey pollution of the seas.
	World population growing by 2% per year, estimated at 3.5 billion.
	225 million telephones in service, 114 million in the United States.
1970	231 million television sets in use worldwide.
	World population in millions: China, 760; India, 550; USSR, 243; U.S., 205.
1973	Energy crisis: oil shortage and embargo cause unemployment and discomfort throughout world.
1974	Smallpox epidemic kills 10,000–20,000 in India.
	Net profits of 30 largest companies increased by 93%.
	South Africa denied UN seat because of apartheid system.
1975	Fifth assembly of World Council of Churches calls for "radical transformation of civilization."
1978	World population: 4.4 billion; 200,000 added daily.
1979	Rise in religious fundamentalism around the world begins to affect world politics.
	Refugees from Vietnam and Cambodia flee their nations in small boats.
1980–1987	African economies suffer as droughts and wars spread.
	People's Republic of China loosens radical Communist stance to experiment with some elements of capitalist development.
	Increasing antinuclear activity throughout the world, partly as a result of the "nuclear winter" theory.
	Deadly gas leaked from storage tank, 1984, killing 2,500 in Bhopal, India; largest industrial accident ever.
	Various sanctions imposed on South Africa because of apartheid system, despite slight loosening of voting restrictions.

Biographies of
Contemporary
Global Figures

3

The burden of present uncertainties and the drastic scope of alternative possibilities that have become apparent in our time oppress the minds of many sensitive people. Yet the unexampled plasticity of human affairs should also be exhilarating. . . . Good and wise men in all parts of the world have seldom counted for more; for they can hope to bring the facts of life more nearly into accord with the generous ideals proclaimed by all—or almost all—the world's leaders.

—*William H. McNeill in* The Rise of the West: A History of the Human Community *(Chicago: University of Chicago Press, 1963)*

IN THIS CHAPTER we present 14 biographies of global actors. Although there has been no attempt to be all-inclusive, the biographies present a wide range of personality and thought. These selections, which note the specialities of each global actor, trace the choices they made as they sought to influence the world around them.

Several generalizations about these people may be made. All were, or are, thoughtful and perceptive individuals. Many have had intellectual training in fields of study outside their current specialities. Most mix idealism with concrete experience and have both profited and suffered from that trying blend. All have taken strong positions based on reasoned arguments as well as impassioned opinion. Each actor has contributed to the development of the modern global system.

James Earl Carter (1924–   )

James Earl Carter, known as Jimmy Carter, was born and has lived much of his life in the small rural community of Plains, Georgia. In

1976 he ran for the U.S. presidency, largely on the basis of his record as a successful governor of the state of Georgia. Carter's experience as a state executive, however, proved insufficient training for the demands of complex national and international issues.

Although Carter floundered on a number of major domestic issues, he achieved several ideological and diplomatic victories in international affairs and the struggle for world peace. Carter, who had come to office on a platform of honest government and assurance of basic human rights, made human rights a key issue in his formulation and conduct of foreign policy. The Carter administration strongly criticized and censured nations that denied human rights to their people. Through foreign policy measures such as curtailment of U.S. aid and personal influence he sought to encourage U.S. allies in Asia, Latin America, and Africa to cease violations of human rights. These efforts, although morally laudable, occasionally strained relations between the United States and its allies. The policy also caused a cooling of relations between the United States and the Soviet Union, which Carter continually denounced for violations of the rights to free speech, press, and religion.

Jimmy Carter's administration capped a gradual improvement of diplomatic relations with the People's Republic of China, begun seven years earlier by Richard Nixon. On January 1, 1979, the United States recognized the People's Republic of China and established full diplomatic relations with that nation. Today, China claims a larger share of U.S. trade than does the Soviet Union.

Perhaps the most significant accomplishment in a troubled presidency was Jimmy Carter's mediation of an international agreement between Egypt and Israel. The two nations, enemies since the formation of the Jewish state in 1948, had fought three wars in the three decades that followed. The relationship between Israel and Egypt and other Arab states was a constant threat to Middle East and world peace during the Carter administration, as it had been for many years.

In 1977, Egyptian President Anwar Sadat became the first Arab leader to recognize the state of Israel and meet with its leaders. In a historic visit to Israel, Sadat called for a peace treaty and normal relations between his own country and Israel.

President Carter became a key player in this historic negotiation when talks between Egypt and Israel began to break down in 1978. Carter invited the two Mideast leaders to the United States to continue their negotiations in the privacy of Camp David, with Carter acting as mediator. During two weeks in September 1978, Carter met with Sadat and Israeli Prime Minister Menachem Begin separately and jointly, encouraging and negotiating with the two leaders through standoffs and stalemates. The Camp David Accords were the result of these talks. The accords outlined the basics of an Egyptian-Israeli peace treaty and the withdrawal of Israeli troops from Egyptian territories occupied since the 1967 and 1973 wars. The accords became a landmark in the struggle for peace in the Middle East.

Jacques Cousteau (1910–   )

Jacques Cousteau's long career has seen landmarks in invention, oceanography, undersea exploration, marine biology and botany, and ecology. Born in Saint-André-de-Cubzac, France, Cousteau was the son of a lawyer who was in the service of an American millionaire. As a result, the family traveled constantly and Cousteau had no permanent home. His formal schooling ended with his graduation from the Ecole Navale, France's national naval academy. He became seriously interested in underwater swimming when he was encouraged to take up swimming as physical therapy to strengthen two broken arms.

In the late 1930s Cousteau began to experiment with underwater breathing apparatus and continued his experimentation throughout World War II. His Aqua-lung, the first of its kind, was first produced commercially in 1946. In 1952 he converted a British World War II minesweeper into an oceanographic research ship, the *Calypso,* and began a four-year oceanographic expedition throughout the world. Among his studies at this time were weather studies and human underwater living experiments conducted in cooperation with NASA, the National Geographic Society, and other institutions.

Cousteau has turned his own concern and fascination with the oceans into a global operation. Since 1956, he has coordinated the Cousteau Group, a global enterprise of over 15 organizations committed to oceanographic research, ecological lobbying, filmmaking, and education. Through his films, books, and especially his television productions, Cousteau has educated millions of people around the world not only about the variety and potential within the ocean's ecosystem, but also about its need for protection and preservation. Cousteau is one of the world's leading proponents of ecological preservation. He also promotes the potential of the oceans for future human survival and growth. In the United States, the Cousteau Society was established to convey Cousteau's message of ecology preservation to the government and the public at large.

Additionally, Cousteau serves as director of the Oceanographic Institute and Museum, secretary-general of the International Commission for the Scientific Exploration of the Mediterranean, and chairman of Eurocean, a collaborative operation of 24 European enterprises that works to explore and preserve the oceans. He has been honored with over eight national and international awards and honorary degrees for his research, inventions, and educational efforts.

Deng Xiaoping (1904–   )

Deng Xiaoping was born in Sichuan province, China. The son of a landowner, Deng attended school within the province and later continued his studies in France. There he joined the Chinese Socialist Youth League and then the Chinese Communist Party.

In 1926, Deng returned to a China in which a weak national government was being threatened both by a national communist movement and by powerful regional and provincial warlords. He took a position as an instructor of political science at the Xian Military and Political Academy.

In 1927, Deng was removed from his teaching post because of his Communist party affiliation. He went to work for the Chinese Communist Party, first as an army organizer and later as political commissar for the army and editor of a Red Army journal. Deng continued to serve the Communist party as a political commissar from the beginning of China's war with Japan in 1937 until its end in 1945.

In 1949, the Chinese Communist Party won a long civil war against the Chinese Nationalist Party, the Guomindang, and assumed control of China. Deng held various positions within the government until his appointment in 1952 as vice premier. He also held key positions within the Communist party leadership and was considered to be one of the leading politicians in the People's Republic of China.

In the mid-1960s the Chinese government and Communist party went through a purification campaign, led by Mao Zedong, to expel capitalist thought and practice. During this process, called the Cultural Revolution, Deng was forced out of government office and political power. He returned to prominence in the late 1970s following the death of Mao and the collapse of the Cultural Revolution.

Since his return to political office in 1977, Deng has led a moderate faction of the Chinese Communist Party, which has, in turn, controlled the national government. Deng's moderates have since the early 1980s led China on a course of modernization and more open political and economic relations with the world. Deng's policy has been one of promoting China's economic growth, even at the compromise of some principles of Communist economics. Deng was one of the architects of the "Four Modernizations" program, which has set a course of improving agriculture, industry, science and technology, and the military. The goal of this national program is to have China achieve the status of a world economic power by the year 2000.

Richard Buckminster Fuller (1895–1983)

The "planet's gentle genius," was one writer's way to describe R. Buckminster Fuller and his impact on the world. Fuller was an engineer, inventor, and philosopher who felt that all human needs and problems could be met through careful planning and the application of appropriate technology.

Fuller was fond of describing how and why he came to view the world in large, system terms. Until he was four years old, he was so cross-eyed and farsighted that he could only perceive the world in terms of large, colored shapes. The purchase of correcting lenses opened the world of detail to him, but the ability to detect larger patterns was always his favored skill. The patterns he went on to detect included patterns of physical nature, patterns of human and social development, and patterns of philosophy.

Among his most famous inventions are the geodesic dome, the Dymaxion house, and the Dymaxion car. The geodesic dome in particular has become common. The domes are constructed of various materials designed to enclose maximum area with minimum weight and to attain maximum strength with minimum material. Fuller's discovery of the natural strength of the pyramid-shaped tetrahedron has been used in thousands of structures around the world.

Seeking to improve the accuracy of world maps, Fuller devised a new method of projecting the round globe onto a flat map in 1943. The

Dymaxion Air-Ocean World Map actually helped set the stage for the discovery of the geodesic dome. The combination of the map and the dome led Fuller to envision a method for forecasting and presolving the problems of the world.

In 1969 he devised a system he called the World Game. This "game" would ideally be played or experienced on a huge model of the entire earth. He suggested that a model roughly the size of the United Nations building in New York could be suspended within sight of the United Nations to provide the perfect location for the game. All aspects of existence on the earth could be illustrated and programmed into the globe using colored lights and computers. By constantly updating world data, the model would in graphic, inescapable detail show exactly where problem areas were developing. Experts could then apply their knowledge to solving the problems. Another application of the game would be to simulate or project possible problems, analyze the resulting interactions on the globe, and prepare responses in case those scenarios actually happened.

As Fuller's fame spread in the 1960s he traveled the world spreading his vision of a world population in harmony with its environment. To illustrate his ideas of the increasing complexity of modern life, he wore three watches on his arm—one so he could keep track of time at his home, one for the location where he was currently speaking or working, and one for the time at his next speaking location. The accelerating pace of invention, and the trend to always do more with less, convinced Fuller that most people were already living better than any king ever lived in 1900. He saw as his task the enhancement of the human environment such that all people could continue to enjoy that degree of progress in the future.

Pope John Paul II (1920–   )

Born in Poland and christened Carolus Joseph Wojtyla, Pope John Paul II followed an early career aspiration to become an actor. His calling toward a religious life came during World War II when Poland was occupied by the Nazis. The German occupation government outlawed religious practice. To keep their religion alive, Wojtyla and other Catholics formed secret prayer groups, which met in defiance of the

Nazis. During this period, Wojtyla made the decision to enter the Catholic priesthood.

Following World War II, Wojtyla continued his studies for the priesthood at Vatican City, the Catholic city-state located in Rome. In 1948 he returned to Poland as Father Karol Wojtyla; his major effort was to help the Polish people recover from the war. By 1964, Wojtyla was named Archbishop of Krakow, Poland; in 1967 he was elevated to the position of cardinal. Throughout his 30 years as a Catholic leader in Poland, Wojtyla was called upon to defend and protect the Catholic religion against a Communist government officially opposed to all religious practice.

In 1979, Wojtyla was elected the first non-Italian pope in over 400 years. He took the name John Paul II. Pope John Paul II's policies as the leader of the global Catholic community are complex. On one level, he has been a revolutionary pope. Traveling more than any pope before him, John Paul II has brought a message of international peace to every continent. He emphasizes personal contact with his Roman Catholic followers and often travels through the crowds in open-air cars, mingling with audiences wherever he goes. His constant contact with the people has earned John Paul II the nickname of the "Pilgrim Pope."

In his travels, John Paul II has expressed frank views on world peace, disarmament, an end to world hunger, and inalienable human rights—stands considered by some observers to cross the bounds between the religious and the political. On another level, John Paul II is conservative, supporting traditional Catholic doctrine such as the permanence of the clerical vows, all-male priesthood, and prohibition of divorce, birth control, homosexuality, and extramarital sex.

Ayatollah Ruhollah Khomeini (1900–   )

Ruhollah Khomeini was born and attended school in Khomein. As a young man, he moved to Qom to study theology, later taking a job at the theological school where he was educated. Ayatollah is an honorific title for a major religious leader in the Islamic religion.

As early as the 1960s, Khomeini opposed the rule of Iran's hereditary ruler, Shah Mohammed Reza Pahlavi. In 1963, Khomeini was involved in riots over the Shah's land reform. Arrested for his role in these riots, Khomeini was exiled by the Iranian government to Turkey.

Between 1964 and 1979, the years of his exile from Iran, Khomeini lived in Turkey, Iraq, and France.

In the late 1970s, opposition to the rule of the Shah of Iran was growing among the Iranian people as well as foreign governments. This opposition was targeted against policies of political and social repression practiced by the government, corruption within the government, and economic policies of westernization and modernization that improved life for only the elite in Iranian society.

In his efforts to achieve rapid modernization, the Shah of Iran enforced policies that often contradicted Islamic traditions and values. To many Moslems, modernization and westernization were perceived as a threat to the Islamic religion. From his exile in France, Khomeini led a growing movement of Moslem fundamentalists who sought a return to strict religious leadership for Iran.

Faced with massive demonstrations and the inevitable collapse of his government, the Shah of Iran fled his country in January 1979. Immediately thereafter, on February 1, 1979, Khomeini returned to Iran to assume leadership of the Islamic revolution taking place there. He was proclaimed Supreme Leader of the Islamic Revolution and Founder of the Islamic Republic of Iran. Khomeini quickly moved to expel modern and foreign influences from Iran and to move that nation toward a social and political code based on strict interpretation of Islamic law.

Khomeini's establishment of a fundamentalist Islamic government in Iran is of global significance. On one level, the Islamic revolution led by Khomeini in Iran quickly became a symbol and a model for the rest of the Islamic world. Khomeini has consciously tried to export the fundamentalist Islamic form of government practiced in Iran to other Moslem nations, particularly those in the Middle East. Khomeini's teachings have become the guidelines for Islamic fundamentalists around the globe.

On another level, Khomeini's rule in Iran has had global economic and political repercussions. Iran, a strong and crucial ally of the United States under the Shah, is now a volatile and nonaligned nation. The country not only exercises a strong influence over the other Islamic nations in the Middle East, it also operates from a strategic location on the Persian Gulf, a main transportation route for Middle Eastern oil headed for Europe and the Americas.

According to Khomeini, the United States—a strong supporter of the Shah of Iran until his overthrow—and other Western nations are a political, social, and ideological threat to the Islamic world. When Khomeini came to power in 1979, his government stopped the production and export of Iranian oil to Western nations. This move was in keeping with Khomeini's efforts to return his nation to Islamic fundamentalism. Because Iran under the Shah had provided 10 percent of the oil of the West, this shutdown began an oil crisis, the second experienced by Western nations in ten years. Now, ten years later, Iran's hostility toward the United States and other nations is a key element in the continuing tension over navigation of the Persian Gulf.

Henry Alfred Kissinger (1923–   )

Heinz Alfred Kissinger—he changed his name to Henry after coming to the United States in 1938—grew up in a cultured, devoutly Jewish middle-class atmosphere in Fürth, Germany. Because of increasing Nazi pressure on the Kissingers, the family emigrated to New York City. While pursuing a degree in accounting, Kissinger was drafted into the United States Army. He became a naturalized citizen in 1943.

Assigned to Europe, he saw action in the Battle of the Bulge. He became interpreter for his commanding general and served as an interrogator with the 970th Counter-Intelligence Corps. Following Germany's surrender in 1945, Kissinger became a district administrator with the military government of occupied Germany. He remained in the Army Military Intelligence Reserve until 1959, attaining the rank of captain.

In 1946 Kissinger returned to the United States and entered Harvard. He obtained his B.A. summa cum laude in 1950. While continuing his education, Kissinger worked as a consultant to the Army Department's Operations Research Office and the Psychological Strategy Board of the Joint Chiefs of Staff. He obtained his M.A. in 1952 and his Ph.D. in 1954. After failing to obtain a tenured position at Harvard, Kissinger headed a research program sponsored by the Council on Foreign Affairs.

This research on alternatives to nuclear war as a means of coping with the Soviet challenge in a nuclear age resulted in his major work *Nuclear Weapons and Foreign Policy* in 1957. In this book he presented the option that Secretary of State John Foster Dulles embraced as "flexible response." Kissinger asserted that strategy must direct technology instead of being determined by available weapons. He did not, however, reject the tactical use of nuclear weapons. For the work he received the Woodrow Wilson Prize and became established as a foremost defense advisor to the highest levels of the government and a leading authority on international relations.

Despite his misgivings about American involvement in Vietnam, Kissinger acted as President Johnson's emissary to secret meetings in Paris with North Vietnamese diplomats that led to the opening of peace talks in 1968. With the election of Richard Nixon in 1968, Kissinger accepted a post as assistant to the president for national security affairs. He became executive secretary of the National Security Council and directed the coordination of foreign, domestic, and military policies pertaining to national security. In 1973 he became secretary of state and held that post until 1977.

Kissinger's diplomatic skills were severely tested during his prominent roles in the negotiations during the Vietnam settlement of January 1973 and the Middle East cease-fires of 1973 and 1974. He was responsible as well for laying the delicate groundwork preceding President Nixon's 1972 visit to China. For his efforts in the Vietnam negotiations he received the 1973 Nobel Peace Prize with Le Doc Tho of North Vietnam. Kissinger has received numerous awards for his diplomatic writings and achievements. He continues to write and serve as an advisor to the government on military and political matters.

Nelson (Rolihlahla) Mandela (1918–   )

In 1964 Nelson Mandela was sentenced to life in prison on charges of sabotage and conspiracy to forcefully overthrow the government of South Africa. Despite having spent the last 24 years behind bars, Mandela is one of the most prominent figures in the black nationalist struggle against South Africa's white minority rule.

Mandela was born in the Transkei territory to a chief of the Xhosa-speaking Tembu tribe. He renounced his hereditary right to succeed his father and sought a career in law and politics. By 1940 Mandela had earned a reputation as a student leader and was expelled from University College at Fort Hare for his role in a student strike. While working as a policeman in the mines of Transvaal, he studied law by correspondence and obtained his degree from the University of South Africa in 1942. Two years later he joined the African National Congress (ANC), South Africa's oldest liberation group.

Following the ideas of Mohandas Gandhi, Mandela sought to use nonviolent actions to correct the injustices of the apartheid system. With Oliver Tambo and others, he formed the Congress Youth League in 1944. This group later dominated the ANC while flirting with various leftist groups. Mandela gradually moved to a position of classic African nationalist socialism that he felt could be attained through a program of nonviolent labor-based pressures on the white government. With the formal institutionalization of apartheid by the National party in 1948, the Youth League responded with a nationwide call for civil disobedience.

In 1952 and 1953 Mandela was "banned" for his role in the campaign of demonstrations and labor strikes. For six months he was prohibited from attending gatherings of any type and confined to Johannesburg. The ban was later extended for two more years. During this period Tambo and Mandela established the first black law partnership in South Africa.

Riots, boycotts, and demonstrations against the government filled 1956. Mandela was among the many Africans arrested and charged under the Suppression of Communism Act. While the trial dragged on into 1961, Mandela divorced his first wife and married Winifred Nomzamo. During the long trial, rifts developed among various groups within the ANC. The splits resulted in the emergence of organizations more willing to take radical actions. On March 21, 1960, thousands of unarmed Africans gathered outside the police station in Sharpeville without their required passbooks. Police turned their guns on the demonstrators, killing 69 and wounding 86. Mandela was detained under a newly proclaimed state of emergency, and held for several months without charges or trial. As a result of the Sharpeville incident, Mandela was convinced that nonviolent resistance was ineffective.

Following his release from detention, Mandela joined the All-African National Action Council and headed the Umkonto we Sizwe, an underground paramilitary group. On August 4, 1962, he was apprehended by South African police in Natal. Conducting his own defense, Mandela challenged the right of the court to hear his case and indicted the entire system of white domination. He was found guilty and sentenced to three years in prison and an additional two years of banning. In 1964 he was tried for his leadership role in Umkonto we Sizwe and sentenced to life in prison.

Recently, the government has slightly relaxed Mandela's nonperson status, although no new photographs have been allowed. In July of 1988 he was transferred from the medical wing of Pollsmoor Prison across

Cape Town to Tygerberg Hospital. There, despite years of a rigorous routine of daily exercise, Mandela was found to be suffering from tuberculosis. Fearing that his death in prison would set off riots, the government provided the best medical attention available.

State President P. W. Botha renewed his offer of release provided that Mandela would renounce the use of violence for political ends and settle quietly in the black homeland of Transkei. Mandela refused the offer on the grounds that prisoners cannot make deals. He continued to hold a socialist, nonracial, democratic South Africa as his primary political goal.

Carl Edward Sagan (1934-   )

The ability to see elements of the minute and the monumental in each item encountered has given Carl Sagan remarkable insight into the workings of the universe. Sagan has translated that complex insight into laymen's terms in numerous works. His range of writings and activities, from musings on the human brain *(Broca's Brain)* to the problems of communication with aliens from space *(Murmurs of Earth* and *Contact)*, were best illustrated in the 1980 television series and companion book, *Cosmos.*

Educated at the University of Chicago and the University of California, Berkeley, Sagan began his academic career as an assistant professor of genetics at Stanford University Medical School. He quickly moved into the fields of astronomy and astrophysics at Harvard University. There the question of the existence of extraterrestrial life and how to communicate with it engrossed him. He served on a joint U.S./USSR panel investigating those problems in 1971.

In 1977 the United States launched two Voyager spacecraft to explore Jupiter and Saturn. Affixed to each of those spacecraft was a gold phonograph record encoded with a myriad of information about Earth and its inhabitants. The Voyager project was a logical outgrowth of Sagan's extensive work on determining just what and how to communicate to aliens. Although actual extraterrestrial contact is unlikely, Sagan included substantial data to characterize the people of Earth. The record contains 117 encoded pictures, greetings in 54 different human languages as well as greetings from the humpback whale, a representative selection of the sounds of Earth, and 90 minutes of some of the world's greatest music.

While addressing an unknown, perhaps nonexistent audience in outer space, Sagan has also continued to focus on the serious implications of his other studies. Sagan was among the first scientists to express concern over the possible "nuclear winter" effect. This event would be a global cooling caused by debris left in the atmosphere after the use of nuclear weapons in an international war. Sagan's recent calculations indicate that as little as 100 megatons of explosive power, or less than one percent of existing stockpiles, might be enough to initiate the nuclear winter effect. Scientists continue to debate the accuracy of the calculations and the logic of the model proposed by Sagan and others.

The Pulitzer Prize was awarded to Sagan in 1978 for his book *The Dragons of Eden: Speculations on the Evolution of Human Intelligence.* He has also authored more than 350 scientific papers.

Andrei Dmitriyevich Sakharov (1921-   )

In the introduction to *Progress, Coexistence and Intellectual Freedom,* Harrison E. Salisbury describes Andrei Sakharov as "Oppenheimer, Teller, and Hans Bethe all rolled into one. . . . a philosopher and social architect on a world scale." Sakharov, a Soviet physicist and social philosopher, is a scientist who is well aware of the consequences of his discoveries on the broader society around him.

The limited information available on his early life indicates only that Sakharov was born in 1921 and graduated with honors in physics from Moscow State University. Under the guidance of Igor Tamm he earned his doctorate at the unusually young age of 26. His academic and theoretical skills had exempted him from military service during World War II.

In 1948 Sakharov published articles outlining the principles for the magnetic thermal isolation of high-temperature plasma, thus altering the course of Soviet research on controlled thermonuclear reactions. Only years later was it revealed that he was a major contributor to the development of the Soviet hydrogen bomb. It has also been established that in 1950 Sakharov and Tamm formulated the theoretical basis for controlled thermonuclear fusion, a process that could lead to the employment of nuclear fusion for the generation of electricity. He was the youngest full member ever elected to the prestigious Soviet Academy of Sciences in recognition of his accomplishments.

During the 1950s and 1960s Sakharov denounced the evils of the repressive regimes of Khrushchev and Brezhnev and protested to officials that the excesses of the Stalin period would not again be tolerated by Soviet citizens. There is some evidence that he may have stopped working on weapons systems in the mid-60s, as the titles of his publications shift to an interest in theoretical studies concerning the structure of the universe. In 1968 the *New York Times* published Sakharov's 10,000-word "manifesto" decrying the political divisions that perpetuated "intellectually simplified, narrow-minded mass myths" that made nations prey to the demagogues of government.

In 1970, with colleagues Andrei N. Tverdokhlebov and Valery N. Chalidze, Sakharov created the Committee for Human Rights, an autonomous, nongovernmental organization that seeks to apply the humanitarian principles of the Universal Declaration of Human Rights within the Soviet Union. As a result, Sakharov suffered a variety of harassments from the government. For his philosophical and humanitarian work he received the Nobel Peace Prize in 1975. Although his scientific work had earned him the Order of Lenin and the Stalin Prize, he was stripped of all Soviet honors in January 1980.

In 1980 Sakharov and his second wife, Yelena Bonner, began a seven-year internal exile to Gorky. On December 17, 1987, they were invited to return to Moscow by Mikhail Gorbachev. While both Sakharov and Bonner suffer from age and ill health, they continue to speak out on human rights, arms control, and cultural restrictions in the Soviet Union. Following the signing of the Intermediate Nuclear Forces agreement, Sakharov publicly commended the action and urged further rapprochement between the people of the United States and the Soviet Union.

Oscar Arias Sanchez (1941–   )

Born near San Jose, Costa Rica, in 1941, Oscar Arias Sanchez comes from one of Costa Rica's most prosperous coffee-producing families. Arias received his early education in Costa Rica and earned a degree in law and economic science at the University of Costa Rica. As a student for a brief time at Boston University in 1960, Arias became an admirer of John F. Kennedy, who was then running for president of the United States.

While at the University of Costa Rica, Arias began his active involvement with the Partido de Liberacion Nacional (the National Liberation Party, PLN), a social democratic party. He worked with the party both in organizing study groups on national affairs and in supporting the PLN candidate in the 1965 presidential election campaign.

Between 1967 and 1969, Arias studied at the University of Essex and the London School of Economics and Political Science under a grant from the British government. He received his doctorate from the University of Essex with a dissertation on the socio-economic origins of the Costa Rican political leadership.

Arias served as a professor of political science at the University of Costa Rica from 1969 until 1972, when he joined the cabinet of Costa Rican President Figueres. As planning minister for the national government, Arias administered a successful program to stimulate national economic growth, technological development, and full employment. Arias continued in the national government in a variety of elected and appointed positions until his election as Costa Rica's youngest president in 1986.

Arias took office as president with the pledge to "keep Costa Rica out of the armed conflicts of Central America and [to] endeavor through diplomatic and political means to prevent Central American brothers from killing each other." Arias emphasized the need for economic recovery in Latin America as well as the importance of maintaining Costa Rica's neutrality.

The nation of Costa Rica plays a critical role in Central American politics. The political situation in Central America, in turn, impacts the rest of the world, particularly the United States and the Western Hemisphere. Among the five nations of Central America, Costa Rica alone has a long and carefully guarded tradition of stable democratic government, as well as a high standard of living for the region. The other nations of Central America have been torn for many years by civil wars, which are often characterized as wars between Communist factions on one side and totalitarian factions on the other. Although the civil wars are generally far more complex than these simple characterizations of two sides, they are perceived as critical disputes in the balance of power between the Soviet and Western bloc countries.

As an anti-Communist, President Arias is a strong critic of Nicaragua's Sandinista government. Yet he also strongly opposes U.S. funding of the anti-Sandinista Contra rebels in Nicaragua on the basis that such support encourages increased support to the Sandinistas by the Soviet Union, ultimately endangering all of Central America.

On February 15, 1987, President Arias proposed a ten-part regional peace plan for Central America. The plan included immediate cease-fires in all guerrilla wars in the region, the suspension of all outside aid to rebel military groups, general amnesty, the beginning of negotiations among all conflicting parties, ultimate free elections, improved human and civil rights in all nations in the region, and a general reduction in military force in the region.

The Arias plan received initial support in Latin America, the United States, and Western Europe. However, within months it came under increasing criticism. Much of this criticism came from the United States, which felt the plan made concessions to the Communist government of Nicaragua and would preclude U.S. aid to the Nicaraguan Contras. Despite U.S. concern, the leaders of the five Central American governments—Guatemala, El Salvador, Nicaragua, Honduras, and Costa Rica—signed a peace plan based on the Arias proposal in August 1987.

Arias was recognized for his efforts to bring peace to Central America by the Nobel Committee, which awarded him the Nobel Peace Prize in 1987.

Mother Teresa (1910–   )

Nearly one thousand members of the Congregation of Charity work with the homeless and dying of the world as a result of the inspiration of Mother Teresa of Calcutta. Beginning in 1950 with a membership of 12, Mother Teresa and her congregation have provided aid and comfort to the world's poorest for nearly 40 years.

Born in what is now Skopje, Yugoslavia, Agnes Gonxha Bojaxhiu knew at an early age that she was destined to work with the poor. At 15 she learned of the huge human needs in India, but waited until she was 18 to join the Sisters of Loretto, a community of Irish nuns with a mission in Calcutta, India. She took her first vows while in training, and finalized them in 1937.

While teaching high school in Calcutta she was struck by the suffering surrounding the cloister. In 1946 she felt a "call within a call" to leave the convent and help the poor while living among them. She attended accelerated medical training for three months then set out with some former students to found the Missionaries of Charity. By 1965 the Vatican recognized the group as a pontifical congregation directly under the jurisdiction of Rome.

In 1952 Mother Teresa began to open centers for the care of the destitute and dying. By 1957 she was offering special treatment for lepers. Her associates are committed to offering "whole-hearted free service to the poorest of the poor." As the body of trained workers expanded, and the mission became more well known, staff and money were found to expand into more than twenty cities and seven nations in the early 1960s.

Mother Teresa has been described as a slight, stooped, unsentimental, down-to-earth bundle of energy. Her charismatic manner has helped her attract recruits and donations for her projects. Malcolm Muggeridge, in his book about her, *Something Beautiful for God,* recalls that her face and demeanor were such that "I knew that, even if I were never to see Mother Teresa again, the memory of her would stay with me forever."

Unaffected by the larger causes of death and poverty that surround her, Mother Teresa is guided by the simple principle of providing as much Christian love as possible to all who seek it. Where some would see an insignificant impact on the immense poverty of India, Mother Teresa seems to see the personal effects of providing love for individual people within her reach and capabilities. For these efforts she has received recognition through the Pope John XXIII Peace Prize, the Templeton Foundation Prize, the Bharat Ratna Star of India, the 1979 Nobel Peace Prize, and several honorary degrees.

Lech Walesa (1943–   )

Massive labor strikes in Poland in July of 1980 catapulted an unemployed electrician known as an incorrigible troublemaker into the international limelight. Lech Walesa, soft-spoken workingman, faithful son of the church, drew 10 million of the nation's 17 million workers into the first independent labor union in the Communist world.

Trained as an electrician, Walesa worked in the shipyards of Gdansk on the Baltic coast. In 1970 the government's raising of food prices sparked violent protests in Gdansk. Fifty-five workers were killed by police during the riots. Continuing over four days, the riots eventually gained the resignation of the Polish Communist party first secretary.

New officials made some concessions to workers, but were unable to sustain worker satisfaction over the long run. By 1976, shortages of meat and other commodities stirred demonstrations in other Polish cities. For his overt support of the protesting workers, and for boldly pointing out the erosion of concessions gained six years previously, Walesa was fired.

The next few years were tight as Walesa worked infrequently because of his reputation as a labor leader. He suffered several job losses and jailings. Although Walesa was a relative moderate, he was strongly influenced by the more radical leanings of the Committee for Social Self-Defense. Through underground bulletins and its newspaper *Robotnik*, this committee served as a communications clearinghouse. Workers who had been laid off could get some relief and help in finding another job, and those interested in leading the swelling discontent could meet together to learn how to channel their needs and ideas.

Two circumstances that significantly helped Poland avert heavier Soviet wrath were the 1975 signing of the Helsinki Agreements and the October 1978 election of Karol Cardinal Wojtyla as the first Polish pope. The Helsinki Agreements helped insure that the Soviet Union would allow some flexibility in dealing with Poland, to use it as a showcase of the new Soviet tolerance. The pope's homecoming tour showed the world the difference between the passion of the Polish people and the coldness of the Polish/Soviet government.

Walesa stepped directly into the labor movement in 1979 with the publication of *The Worker of the Coast*, a bimonthly paper subtitled "the organ of the founding committee of the free trade unions." As a cofounder, he sought an end to censorship, an eight-hour day, improved job safety, higher wages, and legalization of the right to strike. Walesa also stated that strikes were a useful short-term weapon for reminding government to stick to its agreements. When workers at the Lenin Shipyard went on strike on August 14, Walesa became the strike leader. He helped maintain the strike as it expanded into other businesses and other cities until over 300,000 workers were actively engaged in it. On August 31 Walesa signed the Gdansk agreement, granting workers the right to form independent unions and to strike. It was the first such concession in any Soviet bloc country.

Throughout the early 1980s, Walesa has continued to work with labor and government to improve the conditions of Polish workers. In March 1981 Poland's largest strike occurred when most of its 13 million workers protested the beatings of union activists. For his leadership skills, Walesa was reelected chairman of Solidarity. In 1983 Walesa was awarded the Nobel Peace Prize.

Elie Wiesel (1928–   )

Elie Wiesel has been described as "the spiritual archivist of the Holocaust." As a survivor of Auschwitz and Buchenwald, Wiesel has devoted his life to illuminating the Jewish experience and the human needs of all dispossessed persons.

Born in Sighet, Transylvania, near the Ukrainian border, Wiesel spent his early years learning both scholarship and spirituality under his parents' direction. His childhood ended in 1944 when the Nazis deported the entire Jewish population of Sighet to Auschwitz concentration camp in Poland. In the camp his mother and youngest sister died in the gas chambers. In 1945 Wiesel and his father were transported to Buchenwald concentration camp in Germany. His father died there of starvation and dysentery.

Following the liberation of Buchenwald in April of 1945, Wiesel attempted to immigrate to Palestine, but was unable to meet British requirements for certification. Boarding a train filled with orphans, he was placed with a children's aid society. Wiesel learned French and studied literature, psychology, and philosophy at the Sorbonne. In 1948 he became a journalist and traveled widely, reporting for several publications. While reporting on the new United Nations in New York City, he was persuaded to apply for American citizenship.

The Hasidic storyteller tradition of his childhood sparked his ambition to become a writer, but he held to a personal vow not to write about his concentration camp experiences for ten years. In 1956 he published his first book in Yiddish, the language of his childhood. In 1960 it was edited, translated, and published as *Night*. From that point on, Wiesel has written as a survivor and a witness to the atrocities of totalitarian control. This concept of writer as witness made him increasingly aware of the conditions of Jews in the Soviet Union. He is often credited as being a pioneer in the movement to help Jews emigrate from the Soviet Union.

The impact of Wiesel's writing on the world awareness of the Holocaust is difficult to overestimate. Wiesel is said to be the first to use the term "holocaust" in describing the attempted destruction of the Jews. The impulse to testify has been the driving force of his career, yet he has been pained by the trivial manner in which popular film and literature have portrayed the Holocaust experience.

For his writings, Wiesel has received dozens of awards. These honors were capped in 1986 with the Nobel Peace Prize. The committee cited him as "one of the most important spiritual leaders and guides" in an age characterized by "violence, repression, and racism." The United States honored Wiesel by awarding him the Gold Medal of Achievement in recognition of his leadership as chairman of the United States Holocaust Memorial Council, his work in advancing human rights, and his contributions to literature. At the award ceremony, Wiesel tried unsuccessfully to dissuade President Reagan from making a planned visit to an SS cemetery in West Germany. Wiesel reaffirmed his support for a reconciliation with the German people and repeated his opposition to the idea of collective guilt.

World Data

T°O A GREAT EXTENT, recognizing international relationships and acting upon global issues depends on the skills of analyzing and applying both quantitative statistical data and source materials. This chapter contains a variety of illustrations, including tables, charts, and graphs, that are a small sampling of the statistical data from which global relationships, trends, and issues are identified and analyzed. In addition, the chapter contains a small selection of source materials—international treaties and laws—reflecting international agreements, cooperation, and protections, as well as global efforts to address common problems and issues.

The following are some suggestions for reading and interpreting each chart, graph, or map.

1. Read the title. The title states the subject of the data.
2. Note the sources, which may be U.S. government agencies, international organizations, or foreign government agencies.
3. Read the footnotes, if any, as you examine the data. Footnotes provide important additional information needed to read and interpret data accurately.
4. Read the column and row headings. These headings provide details on the type, time span, and category of information.
5. Note the units of measure. Data can be misunderstood if the reader does not identify the exact type of data—e.g., total numbers, percentages, etc.—presented. Be sure to note the size of the numbers presented. Numbers are often presented in thousands or millions, with the zeros omitted.
6. Check the glossary for terms with which you are unfamiliar. Specialized terms that appear in charts and graphs—terms such as gross national product, per

capita, life expectancy, literacy rate, infant mortality rate—are clearly defined in the glossary. Understanding these terms is essential to understanding and applying the data.

7. Examine data for trends, variations, or discrepancies over time or across categories.

Each illustration is discussed briefly below.

Figure 1 presents three timelines reflecting historical events and developments in three major world areas: Europe, the United States, and Japan. The separate presentation of each of these regional or national timelines allows individualized analysis, while the set of three encourages global and cross-cultural comparison of developments and trends. Figure 2, "World Health Catastrophes: A Historical Perspective," is another example of data on the theme of global history. Major epidemics that have affected the world population are identified, as are the locations hardest hit by these epidemics and the number of people killed. Students analyzing this chart should keep in mind that populations were much smaller in earlier centuries and so numbers killed represent a much higher proportion of the total population.

The next four items (Figures 3-6) present a variety of world population data. In Figure 3, world population at two points in recent history is broken down by continent. The inclusion of data on area in square miles for each continent allows the reader to calculate population density, shifts in population density for each continent, and population growth over a 35-year period. Which continents are gaining population? Which are gaining fastest? Which continent experiences the highest population density? Without presenting data on total population, Figure 4 displays the population growth for each continent or region over a 25-year period. Note that the source is the Population Reference Bureau, which provides demographic data on the world as well as the United States. Figure 5 was compiled by using statistics on population growth over time and current birth rates to project population growth to the year 2020. Note that for purposes of this chart, the world has been broken into two categories: Europe, North America, Japan, New Zealand, Australia, and USSR; and Africa, Asia, Latin America, and Oceania. What criteria may have been used to make this categorization? Do the regions and continents within each category have social, political, or economic similarities? Note the difference in the rates of growth of the areas in the two categories. Figure 6 presents a specialized population chart. This chart categorizes the population of five continents and the USSR by 16 religious groupings. The chart may be useful in analyzing the birthplace and spread of religions throughout the world.

Three theme maps (Figures 7–9) reflect the wide range of data that can be presented through maps, as well as the different lenses through which the world can be viewed. In Figure 7, the earth is divided by broken lines into three temperature zones, and countries are presented within one of seven income categories based on annual per capita income in 1985. Students may use this map to focus on global development issues, analyzing income ranges and trends within temperature regions and hypothesizing about such trends, as well as about exceptions. Figure 8 identifies the location of major insect pests and insect-carried diseases throughout the world. In comparing this map to the previous map identifying temperature zones, one sees a strong correlation between temperature and insect pests and diseases. The final map in this set, Figure 9, presents geologic data on earthquake belts, sites of major earthquakes, and active volcanoes.

The next grouping of illustrations (Figures 10–14) uses a variety of formats to illustrate the theme of global environmental systems and issues. Figure 10, "Record Oil Spills," identifies dates, ships, and locations of the accidents, as well as the number of tons of oil spilled. Figure 11 offers a sampling of the animals that are in danger of extinction throughout the world. Figure 12 paraphrases the major points of the 1970 United Nations Declaration of Principles Governing the Seabed, while Figure 13 paraphrases the key elements of the UN Treaty guiding the use and development of the land of Antarctica. Figure 14 maps international claims to the land of Antarctica, which has no native population.

Figure 15, a simple chart, identifies nations that are the principal sources of refugees. The chart does not indicate whether refugees are politically, religiously, or economically motivated, nor does it indicate which nations are offering a haven for these refugees. The chart should serve as a starting place for researching the global problem of refugees.

A bar graph, Figure 16, presents the infant mortality rates of a small selection of countries. The horizontal line on the graph indicates infant deaths per 1,000 live births; the vertical line indicates country. The following bar graph, Figure 17, indicates satellites in space by country. In this case, countries are designated on the horizontal line and number of satellites on the vertical. Note that the arrow pointing above the highest point on the vertical line for the USSR indicates more satellites than can be shown on the graph.

Figure 18 presents an abstract, graphic depiction of nuclear explosive power of the world.

The final set of Figures (19–21) uses a variety of formats to present data on global security and cooperation. Figure 19, a simple chart, details the sites and dates of all summer and winter Olympic games from 1896 through 1988. Figure 20 graphically outlines the organization, councils, and departments of the United Nations, reflecting the flow of authority of each segment of the organization. The final document summarizes the main points of the Universal Declaration of Human Rights, an international agreement adopted by the United Nations in 1948.

Figure 1
History in Global Perspective: Three Timelines

EUROPEAN HISTORY TIMELINE

200-400	Rise of Christianity
449	Angles, Saxons, and Jutes conquer Britain
542	Europe ravaged by bubonic plague
751	Spread of paper-making from China to Europe
774	Charlemagne's conquest of Italy
793	Start of Viking raids
800	Charlemagne crowned emperor in Rome; beginning of new Western (later Holy Roman) empire
900	Start of feudalism in Europe
1066	Norman conquest of England
1095-1291	Crusades
1350	Start of Renaissance
1455	Gutenberg Bible printed
1492	Columbus's voyage to America
1498	India reached by Vasco da Gama
1500-1600	New World claimed by European countries
1588	Spanish Armada defeated by English
1470-1700	Scientific Revolution
1688	Glorious Revolution in England
1750	Beginning of Industrial Revolution
1789	French Revolution
1804	Napoleon crowned Emperor of France
1848	Revolutions in France, Austrian Empire, Italy, Germany
1869	Opening of Suez Canal
1870	Franco-Prussian War and beginning of Age of Imperialism
1914	Start of World War I in Europe
1919	Treaty of Versailles
1929-39	World economic depression
1933	Hitler's rise to power
1939	Start of World War II in Europe
1945	World War II ends in Europe
1947	Marshall Plan
1955	Warsaw Pact/Cold War

Figure 1 *(continued)*

U.S. HISTORY TIMELINE

150-900	Early Indian civilizations, including Mayan Empire in Central America
1492	Columbus's voyage to America
1607	First permanent English settlement in America founded at Jamestown
1619	House of Burgesses established in Virginia
1620	Massachusetts Bay Colony founded
1619-1730	Founding and development of original 13 colonies
1776	Declaration of Independence; United States of America established
1781	British surrender; end of Revolutionary War
1787	Constitution of the United States written
1787-1848	Expansion of United States from Atlantic to Pacific
1846-48	Mexican-American War
1849	California Gold Rush
1853	Trade with Japan opened by Commodore Perry
1860-65	Civil War
1850-1900	Industrialization and urbanization in United States; immigration to United States by Asians
1800s	Asian immigration stopped by U.S. law
1898	Spanish-American War; U.S. colonization in Asia
1914	Start of World War I in Europe
1917	United States entry into World War I
1918	End of World War I; world power status for United States
1924	Passage of immigration law restricting Japanese immigrating to United States and denying immigrants full citzenship
1929-39	Economic depression in the United States
1941	United States entry into World War II following Japanese bombing of Pearl Harbor
1945	Atomic bombing of Hiroshima and Nagasaki by United States
1945	End of World War II
1945-1951	U.S. occupation of Japan

Figure 1 *(continued)*

JAPANESE HISTORY TIMELINE

200-500	Earliest Japanese sculptures, called haniwa
500	First written literature in Japan
607	Buddhist religion introduced into Japan from Korea
645	Features of Chinese government adopted by Japan; central government controlled by an emperor
700	Buddhist temples built in Nara
794	Japanese capital city moved from Nara to Kyoto
900	First university founded at Kyoto
930	Civil war
1020	Japan's great early novel, *Tale of Genji*, completed
1185-1300	Great estates became powerful; lords of estates hired bands of warriors, called *samurai*, to protect their lands
1542	Portuguese traders opened trade with Japan
1603	Tokugawa Ieyasu unified Japan; named *shogun*
1614	All whites expelled from Japan (except Dutch traders in Nagasaki)
1700s	Development of urban Japan; rise of puppet plays, *kabuki*, floating world block prints
1853	Commodore Perry's arrival in Japan to open trade with United States
1868	Meiji restoration; emperor restored as leader of Japan. End of feudalism. Start of modernization
1889	Constitutional monarch—emperor with absolute power
1894	Conquest of Korea
1904	Japanese victory in Russo-Japanese War; Japan a world power
1930	World depression hits Japan
1937	China invaded by Japan
1941	Pearl Harbor bombed by Japan; entry of Japan into World War II
1945	Atomic bombings of Hiroshima and Nagasaki
1945	End of World War II
1945-51	U.S. occupation

Source: Jacquelyn Johnson and Lynn S. Parisi, *Japan in the Classroom* (Boulder, CO: Social Science Education Consortium, Inc., 1987).

Figure 2
World Health Catastrophes: A Historical Perspective

Epidemics

1347-1350:   *Bubonic Plague.* Killed 17 million to 28 million
                     people—one-third to one-half of Europe's
                     population.

1800's: *Smallpox.* Killed 400,000 Europeans at the
                     height of the epidemic.

1917-1918:   *Influenza.* Killed 22 million.

1943-1956:   *Polio.* Killed 22,000 Americans of 400,000
                     infected.

1981-1987:   *AIDS.* World Health Organization estimates
                     73,000 cases of AIDS since 1981 and possible
                     5-30 million deaths by 2000.

Other Causes of Death

Measles   Kills at least 1.5 million people worldwide each year.

Tuberculosis   Kills 500,000 people worldwide each year.

Pregnancy and   Kill 500,000 women worldwide each year.
Childbirth

Ethiopian Famine   Killed 1 million people during 1984-85.

Source: Data from Lori Heise, "AIDS: New Threat to the Third World," *World Watch*, Vol. 1,
No. 1 (January–February 1988), p. 20.

Figure 3
Area and Population of the World by Continent

Continent	Area (thousands of sq. miles)	Population (thousands)	
		1950	1985
Africa	11,700	199,000	538,000
Asia	17,250	1,418,000	2,946,000
Antarctica	5,400	uninhabited	uninhabited
Australia/Oceania	3,300	13,000	24,200
Europe	3,800	530,000	673,900
North America	9,400	219,000	397,400
South America	6,900	111,000	263,300

Source: Data from Edward Espenshade, Jr., ed., *Goode's World Atlas,* 17th ed. (Chicago: Rand McNally and Co., 1986), pp. 241–245.

Figure 4
World Population Growth

| Continent | Annual Percentage Rate of Growth | | |
or Region	1960-70	1970-80	1980-85
Africa	2.45%	2.70%	2.90%
Asia	2.25%	2.10%	1.80%
Australia/New Zealand	1.95%	1.35%	1.55%
Europe	.80%	.50%	.30%
Latin America	2.75%	2.45%	2.30%
North America	1.30%	1.10%	.90%
Soviet Union	1.25%	.90%	.90%

Source: Data from Population Reference Bureau, *1987 World Population Data Sheet*
(Washington, DC: Population Reference Bureau, 1987).

Figure 5
Population Projections (in millions) to the Year 2020

Year	World	Europe, North America, Japan, New Zealand, Australia, USSR	Africa, Asia, Latin America, Oceania
1950	2,525	832	1,693
1960	3,037	945	2,092
1970	3,695	1,047	2,648
1980	4,432	1,131	3,301
1990	5,242	1,206	4,036
2000	6,119	1,272	4,847
2010	6,988	1,321	5,667
2020	7,813	1,360	6,453

Source: United Nations, Department of International Economic and Social Affairs, *World Population Prospects as Assessed in 1980.* Population Studies, no. 78 (ST/ESA/SER.A/78). 1981.5.

Figure 6
Estimated Religious Population of the World

Religion	Asia	Africa	Europe	Latin America	North America	USSR	World
Christian	221,711,910	259,544,680	415,529,010	388,863,450	231,539,720	102,083,790	1,619,272,560
Muslim	559,316,470	237,067,660	9,042,340	625,180	2,675,720	31,494,020	840,221,390
Nonreligious	640,630,060	1,433,850	48,788,900	12,751,380	19,310,020	82,981,670	805,895,880
Hindu	644,512,180	1,395,390	585,540	636,340	764,200	1,300	647,894,950
Buddhist	306,152,450	13,850	209,600	496,980	193,440	349,710	307,416,030
Atheist	139,174,290	234,470	17,153,270	2,388,410	1,029,120	60,562,030	220,541,590
Chinese Folk	202,510,680	10,220	50,350	68,460	116,160	100	202,755,970
Tribal Religions	26,073,240	70,170,270	50	1,168,160	65,210	0	97,476,930
Jewish	3,981,300	276,390	1,520,060	976,230	8,050,100	3,177,380	17,981,460
Sikh	15,904,900	29,110	212,240	5,950	8,660	50	16,160,910
Shamanist	12,840,820	1,100	300	500	290	299,750	13,142,760
Confucian	5,637,380	550	990	500	1,020	200	5,640,640
Baha'i	2,329,000	1,319,350	67,090	543,460	300,110	4,900	4,563,910
Shinto	3,424,750	50	390	990	710	100	3,426,990
Jain	3,306,060	49,980	9,870	1,980	2,040	20	3,369,950
Other	108,369,530	75,480	329,610	7,082,840	1,710,100	5,200	117,572,760
Total	2,895,875,020	571,622,400	493,499,610	415,610,810	265,766,620	280,960,220	4,923,334,680

Source: Developed from United Nations data by David B. Barrett. Adapted from David B. Barrett, "Adherents of All Religions," *1988 Britannica Book of the Year* (Chicago: Encyclopaedia Britannica, 1988), p. 303.

Figure 7
Temperature and Income

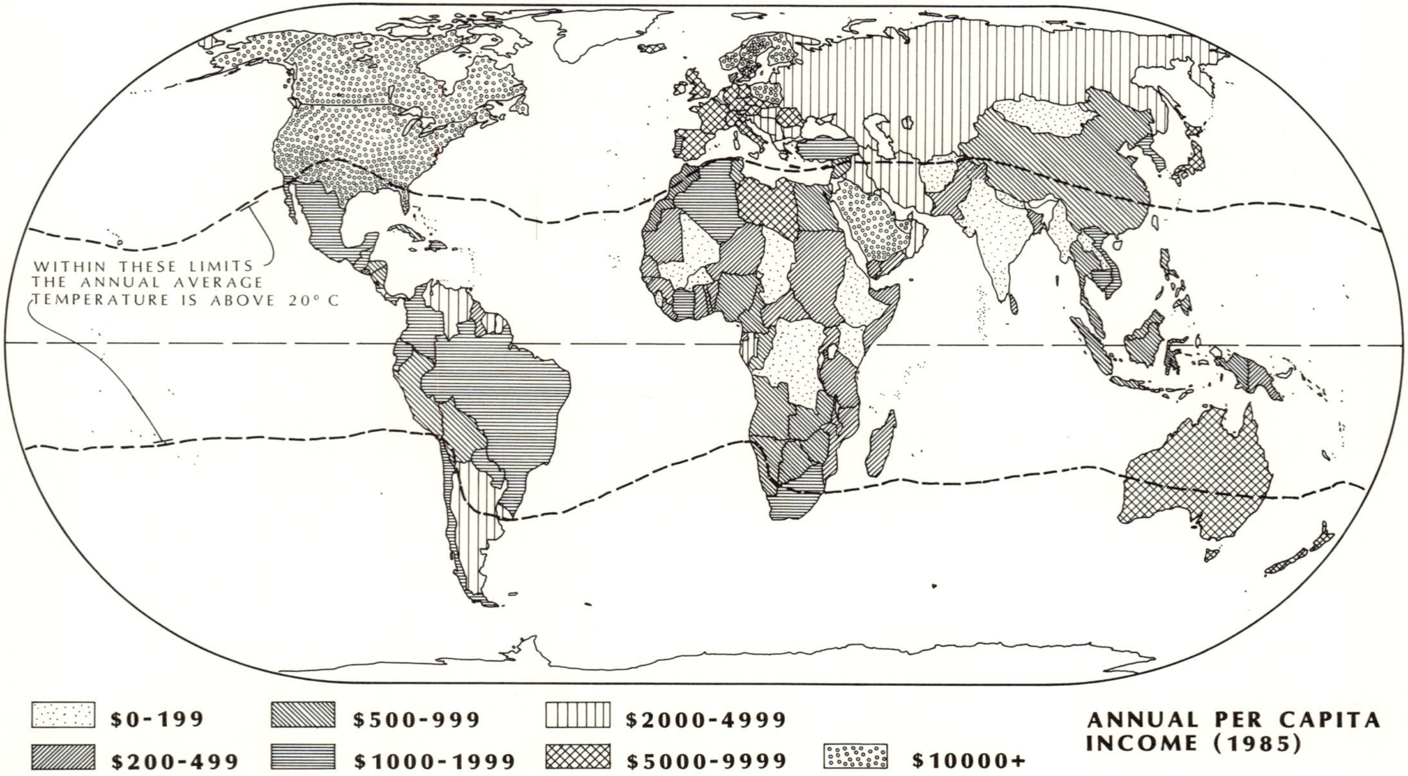

WITHIN THESE LIMITS
THE ANNUAL AVERAGE
TEMPERATURE IS ABOVE 20° C

ANNUAL PER CAPITA
INCOME (1985)

$0-199

$200-499

$500-999

$1000-1999

$2000-4999

$5000-9999

$10000+

Source: Map by Randall J. LaRue. Copyright Randall J. LaRue; used with permission.

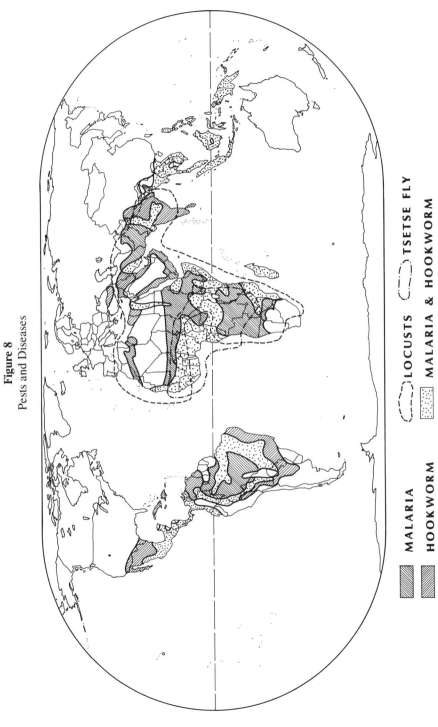

Figure 8
Pests and Diseases

MALARIA

HOOKWORM

LOCUSTS

TSETSE FLY

MALARIA & HOOKWORM

Source: Map by Randall J. LaRue. Copyright Randall J. LaRue; used with permission.

Figure 9
The Unsettled Earth

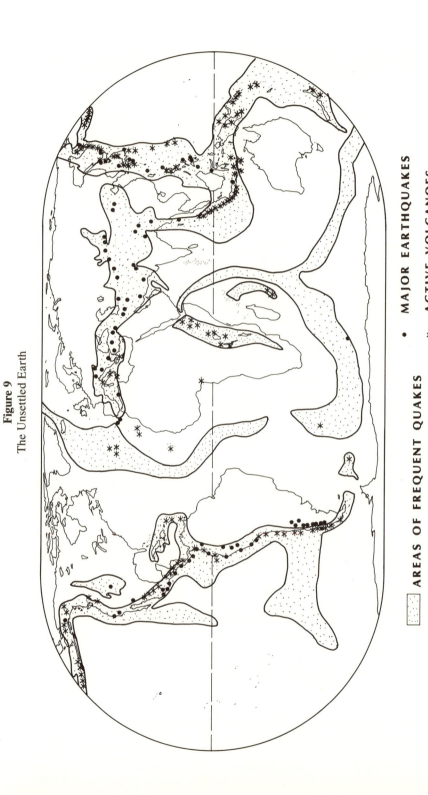

☐ **AREAS OF FREQUENT QUAKES**

• **MAJOR EARTHQUAKES**

✳ **ACTIVE VOLCANOES**

Source: Map by Randall J. LaRue. Copyright Randall J. LaRue; used with permission.

Figure 10
Record Oil Spills

Oil spills have been a serious problem in the past 30 years. They constitute international problems because, as is usually the case, the ships, owned by one nation, develop the leaks while en route from the Middle East to Europe, Asia, or the Americas. The oil leaks affect beaches and marine life in locations removed from either the source or the ultimate destination of the oil.

Date	Name/Place	Tons of oil spilled
March 18, 1967	Torrey Canyon, off England	119,000
March 20, 1970	Othello, off Sweden	80,000
February 27, 1971	Wafra, off South Africa	63,000
December 19, 1972	Sea Star, Gulf of Oman	115,000
January 29, 1975	Jacob Maersk, off Portugal	84,000
May, 1975	Epic Colacotroni, in Caribbean Sea	57,000
May 12, 1976	Urquiola, La Corona, Spain	100,000
February 25, 1977	Hawaiian Patriot, Northern Pacific Ocean	99,000
March 16, 1978	Amoco Cadiz, off coast of France	223,000
July 19, 1979	Atlantic Empress and Aegean Captain, off Trinidad	600,000 (est.)
August 6, 1983	Castillo de Beliver, off Cape Town, South Africa	600,000

Source: Data from *The World Almanac and Book of Facts, 1987* (New York: Ballantine Books, 1986), p. 535.

Figure 11
Selective List of Endangered and Threatened Species, 1986

Common name	Location
American crocodile	United States and Latin America
Asian elephant	Central and East Africa
Bactrian camel	China and Mongolia
Canadian goose	United States and Japan
Giant panda	China
Gorilla	Central and West Africa
Grey whale	North Pacific Ocean
Grizzly bear	United States
Hooded crane	Japan and Soviet Union
Howler monkey	Latin America
Mountain zebra	South Africa
Tiger	Asia
Whooping crane	Canada, United States, Mexico
Wild yak	China, India, and Tibet

Source: Data from *The World Almanac and Book of Facts, 1987* (New York: Ballantine Books, 1986), p. 153.

Figure 12

United Nations Declaration of Principles Governing the Seabed

On the basis of the work of the Seabed Committee, the General Assembly of the United Nations in 1970 adopted unanimously the Declaration of Principles governing the seabed and ocean floor. Some of the major points may be summarized as follows:

1. The seabed and ocean floor, and the subsoil thereof, beyond the limits of national jurisdiction, as well as the resources of the area, are the common heritage of mankind; the area is not subject to appropriation and no state may claim or exercise sovereignty or sovereign rights over any part thereof; no state or person shall claim, exercise or acquire rights with respect to the area or its resources incompatible with the international regime to be established and the principle of this declaration;

2. The area is open to use exclusively for peaceful purposes;

3. The exploration of the area and exploitation of its resources are to be carried out for the benefit of mankind as a whole;

4. States shall act in the area in accordance with the applicable principles and rules of international law, including the UN Charter, and in the interests of maintaining international peace and promoting international cooperation and mutual understanding.

It is the first time in history that the concept of common heritage has found expression in an international instrument. It is perhaps even more significant that an area of at least 225 million square kilometers is reserved for mankind as a whole and will be administered by an international organization on its behalf.

Source: United Nations.

Figure 13
The Antarctic Treaty of 1959

In 1959, 12 nations from around the world agreed on a treaty for the future of Antarctica. These 12 nations were Argentina, Australia, Belgium, Chile, France, Japan, New Zealand, Norway, South Africa, the Soviet Union, the United Kingdom, and the United States. Six other nations later signed the treaty. They are East Germany, Poland, Brazil, India, China, and Uruguay.

The treaty says:

1. Antarctica shall be used only for peaceful purposes.

2. Antarctica is open to scientific investigation.

3. Countries that sign this treaty will share plans, scientific findings, and scientists whenever possible.

4. No new claims to ownership of Antarctica can be made.

5. Nuclear explosions and tests are not allowed in Antarctica.

6. Dumping of nuclear waste is not allowed in Antarctica.

7. The treaty applies to all land areas south of 60 degrees South latitude.

8. In 1991, this treaty can be renegotiated if any one of the treaty signers requests it.

Figure 14
National Claims to Antarctica

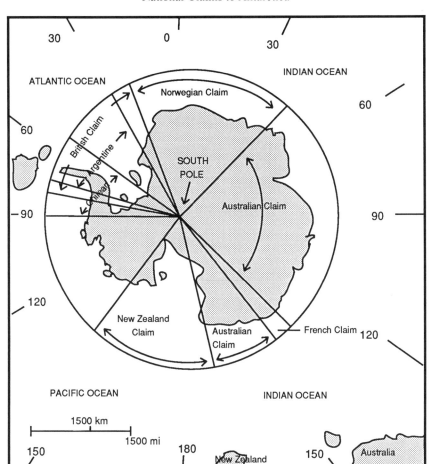

Note: Although Antarctica has no native population, seven nations claim ownership of part of this continent. The 1959 Antarctic Treaty represents an international agreement by eighteen nations to preserve free access to Antarctica for scientific purposes.

Source: Based on data from *National Geographic,* Vol. 171, No. 4 (April 1987), pp. 556–560.

81

Figure 15
Principal Sources of Refugees, 1985

Afghanistan	3,485,000
Palestinians	2,093,500
Ethiopia	1,286,500
Angola	358,000
Cambodia	283,800
Uganda	282,100
El Salvador	251,700
Mozambique	219,100
Rwanda	187,100
Chad	176,300
Burundi	163,500
Western Sahara	165,000
Iran	121,200

Source: Data from *The World Almanac and Book of Facts, 1987* (New York: Ballantine Books, 1986), p. 635.

Figure 16

Infant Mortality Rates, 1985: Selected Countries (infant deaths per 1,000 live births)

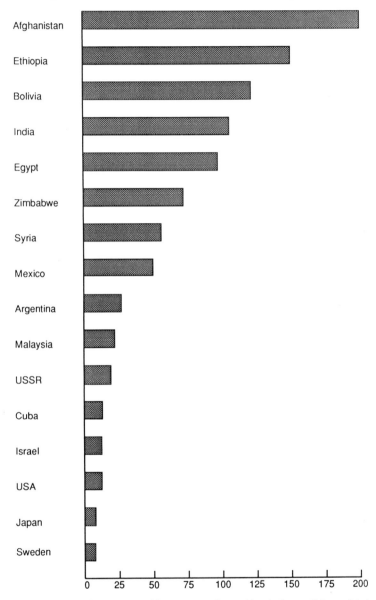

Note: Infants (children under one year old) are extremely sensitive to the conditions of their environment; nutrition, water potability, sanitation, health care, and disease all affect survival of newborns. Thus, the rate of infant mortality within a country is often used as an indicator of that country's general health conditions or its state of socioeconomic development.

The average infant mortality rate (IMR) is 15 infant deaths per 1,000 live births in more developed countries and 86 infant deaths per 1,000 live births in less developed countries.

Source: Data from James P. Grant, *The State of the World's Children, 1987* (Oxford: Oxford

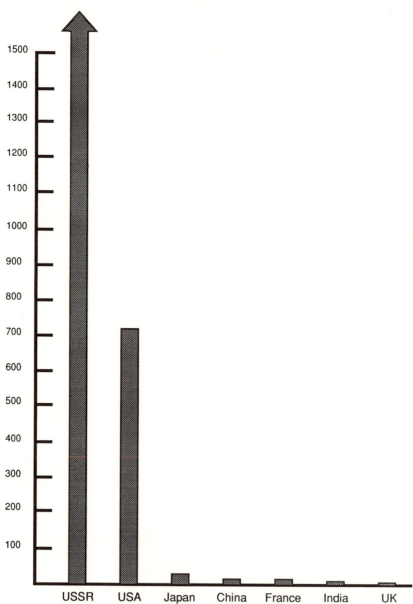

Figure 17
Satellites in Space by Country, 1983

Source: International Cooperation and Competition in Civilian Space Activities (Washington, DC: Congress of the United States, Office of Technology Assessment, July 1985).

Figure 18
Nuclear Explosive Power

☐ A single dot represents all the firepower of World War II: 3 megatons

☐ Three dots represent the firepower of one Poseidon submarine: 9 megatons

☐ Eight dots represent the firepower of one Trident submarine: 24 megatons

☐ One hundred dots represent enough firepower to destroy every major city in the northern hemisphere: 300 megatons

☐ Five thousand, nine hundred and fifty dots represent current world firepower: 17,850 megatons

Source: Data from Teena Mayers, *Understanding Nuclear Weapons and Arms Control: A Guide to the Issues* (Arlington, VA: Education in World Issues, 1984), pp. 27, 33, 42, 45, 49, 51, 52, and 53.

Figure 19
Olympiad Sites and Dates

Summer Games

1. Athens, Greece	1896
2. Paris, France	1900
3. St. Louis, Missouri, USA	1904
4. London, England	1908
5. Stockholm, Sweden	1912
6. Berlin, Germany	Not celebrated: World War I
7. Antwerp, Belgium	1920
8. Paris, France	1924
9. Amsterdam, Netherlands	1928
10. Los Angeles, California, USA	1932
11. Berlin, Germany	1936
12. Tokyo, Japan	Not celebrated: World War II
13. London, England	Not celebrated: World War II
14. London, England	1948
15. Helsinki, Finland	1952
16. Melbourne, Australia	1956
17. Rome, Italy	1960
18. Tokyo, Japan	1964
19. Mexico City, Mexico	1968
20. Munich, Germany	1972
21. Montreal, Canada	1976
22. Moscow, USSR	1980
23. Los Angeles, California, USA	1984
24. Seoul, Korea	1988

Figure 19 *(continued)*

Winter Games

1. Chamonix, France	1924
2. St. Moritz, Switzerland	1928
3. Lake Placid, New York, USA	1932
4. Garmisch-Partenkirchen, W. Germany	1936
5. St. Moritz, Switzerland	1948
6. Oslo, Norway	1952
7. Cortina d'Ampezzo, Italy	1956
8. Squaw Valley, California, USA	1960
9. Innsbruck, Austria	1964
10. Grenoble, France	1968
11. Sapporo, Japan	1972
12. Innsbruck, Austria	1976
13. Lake Placid, New York, USA	1980
14. Sarajevo, Yugoslavia	1984
15. Calgary, Canada	1988

Source: United States Olympic Committee.

Figure 20
The United Nations System

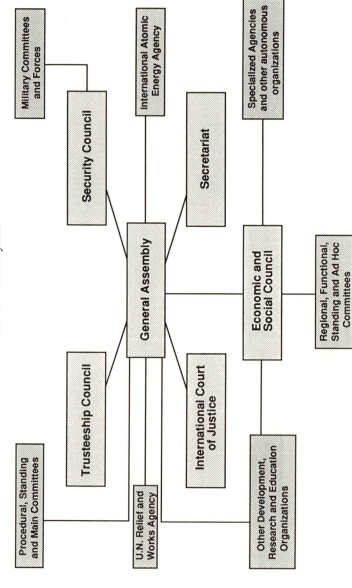

Source: Developed from information in the United Nations Charter. See, for example, Bradford Chambers, *Follett Vest-Pocket Handbook on the United Nations* (Chicago: Follett Publishing Company, 1985).

Figure 21

Universal Declaration of Human Rights, adopted by the United Nations, 1948

1. All human beings are born free and equal in dignity and rights.

2. Everyone has the right to life, liberty, and the security of person.

3. No one shall be held in slavery. . . .

4. No one shall be subjected to torture or to cruel, inhuman, or degrading treatment or punishment.

5. All are equal before the law and are entitled without any discrimination to equal protection of the law.

6. No one should be subjected to arbitrary arrest, detention, or exile.

7. Everyone is entitled in full equality to a fair and public hearing by an independent and impartial tribunal . . . .

8. Everyone charged with a penal offense has the right to be presumed innocent until proved guilty according to law in a public trial at which he has had all the guarantees necessary for his defense.

9. No one shall be subjected to arbitrary interference with his privacy, family, home, or correspondence, nor to attacks upon his honor and reputation.

10. Everyone has the right to freedom of movement and residence within the borders of each State.

11. Everyone has the right to leave any country, including his own, and to return to his country.

12. No one shall be arbitrarily deprived of his nationality nor denied the right to change his nationality.

13. Men and women of full age, without any limitation due to race, nationality, or religion, have the right to marry and to found a family.

14. The family is the natural and fundamental group of society and is entitled to protection by society and the State.

15. Everyone has the right to own property. . . .

16. Everyone has the right to freedom of thought, conscience, and religion. . . .

17. Everyone has the right to freedom of opinion and expression. . . .

18. Everyone has the right to freedom of peaceful assembly and association.

continued

Figure 21 *(continued)*

19. Everyone has the right to take part in the government of his country, directly or through freely chosen representatives. . . .

20. Everyone has the right to work, to free choice of employment, to just and favorable conditions of work and to protection against unemployment.

21. Everyone, without any discrimination, has the right to equal pay for equal work.

22. Everyone who works has the right to just and favorable remuneration.

23. Everyone has the right to form and to join trade unions for the protection of his interests.

24. Everyone has the right to rest and leisure, including reasonable limitation of working hours and periodic holidays with pay.

25. Everyone has the right to a standard of living adequate for the health and well-being of himself and of his family. . . .

26. Motherhood and childhood are entitled to special care and assistance.

27. Everyone has the right to education. Education shall be free, at least in the elementary and fundamental stages. Elementary education shall be compulsory.

28. Everyone has the right freely to participate in the cultural life of the community, to enjoy the arts and to share in scientific advancement and its benefits.

Source: United Nations.

Directory of Organizations, Associations, and Government Agencies

AFS International/Intercultural Programs
313 East 43rd Street
New York, NY 10017
(212) 949-4242
Alan Nierenberg, Vice President for Program Services

AFS is a nonprofit, nongovernmental organization that offers U.S. teachers and students the opportunity to develop a profound understanding of a new culture and country through international exchange and homestay experience. Sample countries with which exchange programs are offered are Argentina, Chile, Costa Rica, Peru, China, Thailand, and the Soviet Union. AFS also seeks U.S. host families for foreign visitors.

PUBLICATIONS: AFS offers publications on contemporary international issues as well as handbooks for cross-cultural programs and encounters. Sample titles in the former category include *Nuclear Mapping Kit; Watermelons Not War: A Support Book for Parenting in the Nuclear Age; Hunger on Spaceship Earth Simulation Game;* and *Changing Course: Blueprint for Peace in Central America and the Caribbean.* In the latter category AFS publishes an annual *AFS Orientation Handbook,* which provides resources for group orientations and for volunteers involved in cross-cultural living experiences.

Alliance for Education in Global and International Studies (AEGIS)
c/o AEGIS Secretariat
45 John Street
New York, NY 10038

Launched in 1988, AEGIS is a consortium of U.S. organizations, programs, projects, and institutions working to enhance the international dimensions of all curriculum areas of elementary and secondary education. Member organizations are provided with networking, staff development, technical support, and evaluation assistance.

PUBLICATIONS: No publications at present; however, a journal is planned.

American Council on the Teaching of Foreign Languages (ACTFL)
579 Broadway
Hastings-on-Hudson, NY 10706
(914) 478-2011
C. Edward Scebold, Executive Director

A national membership association, the ACTFL promotes the teaching of foreign languages at all grade levels. Annual membership dues range from $20 a year for students to $35 a year for regular members. The council operates a materials center and disseminates information about the teaching of foreign languages in the United States. It also conducts workshops, national conferences, and consultations.

PUBLICATIONS: A journal, *Foreign Language Annals,* is free with membership. The council also publishes a newsletter and the *ACTFL Foreign Language Series.*

American Forum: Education in a Global Age
45 John Street
Suite 1200
New York, NY 10038
(212) 732-8606
Andrew Smith, President

The American Forum is an organization formed by the merger in 1987 of Global Perspectives in Education, Inc., and the National Council on Foreign Language and International Studies. It is a nonprofit organization dedicated to increasing U.S. competence in world affairs through education in international studies. The forum works through associations, schools, local and state education agencies, and institutions of higher education to develop materials and programs to prepare students for national citizenship in a global age.

PUBLICATIONS: In addition to a periodic newsletter, *ACCESS,* the American Forum offers an extensive publications list, which includes curriculum materials, research reports, and policy statements. Sample titles include *Next Steps in Global Education: A Handbook for Curriculum Development; Education in a World of Change: A Report; The New Global Yellow Pages; The Global Resource Book; Introduction to International Trade; Simulations for a Global Perspective;* and *Global Education and International Exchange.*

American Institute for Foreign Study Scholarship Foundation (AIFS)
100 Greenwich Ave.
Greenwich, CT 06830
(203) 625-0755
Paul Cook, Executive Director

AIFS was established in 1968 to promote cross-cultural and international understanding through student exchanges. Annually, several hundred teenagers from around the world visit the United States, living with American families and attending American schools. The foundation also offers homestay experiences in Asia and Europe for U.S. high school students.

PUBLICATIONS: None.

Arkansas International Center
University of Arkansas at Little Rock
Little Rock, AR 72204
(501) 569-3282
Walter Nunn, International Education Director

The Arkansas International Center offers services to promote and enhance global education in Arkansas elementary and secondary schools. These services include inservice teacher training programs for senior high school social studies teachers, a high school level student exchange program, and an adult international visitor program.

PUBLICATIONS: The center publishes a quarterly newsletter as well as several publications for educational and general audiences, including *Arkansas: A Guide for International Visitors*, *Arkansas International Directory*, and *International Student Exchange Programs in Arkansas.*

ASSE International Student Exchange Programs
228 North Coast Highway
Laguna Beach, CA 92651
(714) 497-6529
Susan J. Hayes, Regional Director

Originally founded by the government of Sweden as the American Scandinavian Student Exchange (ASSE), these programs operate high school student exchanges between the United States, Canada, Australia, New Zealand, Sweden, Norway, Denmark, Finland, France, Germany, Spain, Switzerland, Great Britain, Holland, and Iceland. Summer and academic year programs are available, as are one-month language study/tour programs. The programs also seek host families for foreign students in the United States.

PUBLICATIONS: None.

Associates in Multicultural and International Education (AMIE)
P.O. Box 14256
Chicago, IL 60614
(312) 472-1531
Marilyn Turkovich, Director

AMIE is a nonprofit organization committed to furthering education that is multicultural and global in focus. AMIE creates curriculum materials and audiovisual materials for schools. It also provides consulting services and conducts workshops on a wide variety of topics.

PUBLICATIONS: AMIE materials are interdisciplinary and activity oriented. Titles include *Omiyage: Japanese Language and Culture*; *Experiencing Indian Languages*; *Nepal: From Kathmandu to Everest*; and *Sri Lanka Learning Center Ideas.*

Association for Supervision and Curriculum Development (ASCD)
225 North Washington Street
Alexandria, VA 22314
(703) 549-9110
Gordon Cawelti, Executive Director

ASCD is a national membership organization dedicated to the dissemination and assimilation within the educational community of innovative concepts, ideas, and curriculum development related to supervision and instruction. The association sponsors an annual national conference, publications, a variety of special interest networks, and an annual program of workshops and seminars in curriculum study, which are conducted around the United States.

PUBLICATIONS: ASCD offers an extensive list of publications. The association's journal, *Educational Leadership,* is available with membership or by separate subscription. ASCD also publishes a yearbook, a newsletter, and volumes on current educational topics. Titles related to global education include *Global Studies: Problems and Promises for Elementary Teachers*; *Education for Peace: Focus on Mankind*; and *Handbook of Basic Citizenship Competencies.*

The Atlantic Council of the United States
Successor Generation Program
1616 H Street, NW
Washington, DC 20006
(202) 347-9353
James R. Huntley, President

Through its "Successor Generation Program," the Atlantic Council seeks to encourage an educational focus on the common heritage and values of Western civilization and the principles of democracy. Among its programs and services are the establishment of an international network of political, economic, media, and educational leaders concerned with education about Western civilization; the operation of an information clearinghouse; curriculum development; materials dissemination; and national and international conferences.

PUBLICATIONS: The Atlantic Council publishes a quarterly journal and a periodic newsletter. Two publications detail the work of the Successor Generation Program: *The Successor Generation: Its Challenges and Responsibilities* and *The Teaching of Values and the Successor Generation.*

AYUSA International
1075 Battery Street
San Francisco, CA 94111
(415) 434-1212
John F. Wilhelm, President

AYUSA (Academic Year in the U.S.A.) operates a high-school year in the United States program for students from Denmark, England, Finland, France, West Germany, Malaysia, Mexico, the Netherlands, Norway, the Philippines, Spain, Sweden, Thailand, and Hong Kong. Students may come to the United States for either an academic year or a semester. Outbound programs for U.S. students are also available.
PUBLICATIONS: None.

California International Studies Project
Littlefield Center, Room 14
300 Lasuen Street
Stanford University
Stanford, CA 94305-5013
(415) 725-1494
Ron Herring, Project Manager

The California International Studies Project is a legislatively enacted effort to improve California elementary and secondary school students' knowledge of international issues, world cultures, and foreign languages. The project is composed of international studies organizations, resource centers, managing and governance structures, and a state agency with oversight responsibility. Member projects and organizations, which serve all the school districts of California, include the Bay Area Global Education Program, International Studies Education Project of San Diego, North Bay International Studies Project, Project in International and Multicultural Education, Southcoast International Resource Center, and Western States International Studies Consortium.

PUBLICATIONS: Many of the organizations and projects within the California International Studies Project conduct publications programs and offer newsletters.

Center for Teaching International Relations (CTIR)
University of Denver
Graduate School of International Studies
Denver, CO 80208
(303) 871-3106
Ronald Shukar, Director

The goal of CTIR is to enhance the teaching of intercultural, international, and current affairs at the elementary and secondary levels. To further this goal, CTIR offers graduate courses in education and teacher inservice workshops through the University of Denver, offers a program leading to a Master of Arts in Curriculum Instruction and International Relations, provides consultation services to school districts, and develops and disseminates curriculum materials through a publications program. Each summer, CTIR conducts an institute for educators on a specific topic in international education. CTIR services and projects are both statewide and national in scope.

PUBLICATIONS: CTIR has an extensive publications program, containing over 30 titles. Publications are predominantly activity and resource books for elementary and secondary teachers. Titles include *Changing Images of China*; *Japan Meets the West: A Case Study in Perceptions*; *Teaching About World Cultures*; *Teaching About the Consumer and the Global Marketplace*; *Teaching About Human Rights*; and *Teaching About Food and Hunger.*

Coalition for the Advancement of Foreign Languages and International Studies (CAFLIS)
One DuPont Circle
Suite 710
Washington, DC 20036
(202) 778-0819
Lillian Pubillones, Executive Director

The rationale for CAFLIS, formed in 1987, is based on the fact that the U.S. position in the world requires high and broadly based competence in languages and knowledge of the cultures and social arrangements of the world. CAFLIS serves as a forum for debate on the steps that need to be taken in order to build and maintain critical international competence.
PUBLICATIONS: None.

Constitutional Rights Foundation (CRF)
601 S. Kingsley Drive
Los Angeles, CA 90005
Russ Donnelly, International Programs

CRF supports a special program on "International Law in a Global Age," through which materials are developed and disseminated and teacher training programs are offered. CRF also serves as the secretariat for the Western States International Studies Consortium, which provides teacher training and resources on international education as well as conferences for students in southern California.

PUBLICATIONS: Curriculum units and activity books on legal traditions around the world, international law, U.S.-USSR trade, and South Africa are available.

Council of Chief State School Officers
400 North Capitol Street, NW
Suite 379
Washington, DC 20001
(202) 393-1228
William F. Pierce, Executive Director

The Council of Chief State School Officers is a membership organization composed of state commissioners and superintendents of education throughout the United States. The Council works to strengthen education through cooperative action among state education agencies. The Council maintains an Office of International Education, which provides inservice teacher training and international program activities, conducts national and international conferences for chief state school officers, maintains a network of state international education representatives, and disseminates materials and information related to international education.

PUBLICATIONS: Resource publications of the council include *The Japan Database* and *Position Paper on International Dimensions of Education* as well as an electronic mailbox, *Chief Line,* which is updated twice weekly.

Council on International and Public Affairs
777 United Nations Plaza
New York, NY 10017
(212) 972-9877
David Dembo, Program Coordinator

A nonprofit organization, the council is devoted to research, education, and publishing to further public understanding of issues and relationships among people of the United States and other nations. The Council conducts conferences, seminars, and workshops, and produces publications under independent programs such as Policy Study Associates, the Center for International Training and Education, and Citizen Participation in Public and International Affairs.

PUBLICATIONS: A catalog is available on request.

Council on International Educational Exchange (CIEE)
205 East 42nd Street
New York, NY 10017
(212) 661-1414
Jack Egle, President/Executive Director

CIEE encourages and facilitates international education through a variety of programs aimed primarily at students and youth. CIEE offers low cost transportation and study programs, work and volunteer abroad programs, language training, sister school relationships, and scholarship funds for U.S. students. The program also offers consultation and planning assistance for educational programs for adults, particularly teachers.

PUBLICATIONS: The Council annually publishes the *Student Travel Catalog* as well as a monthly newsletter of program activities and work-study-travel opportunities, *Campus Update.*

Council on Standards for International Educational Travel
1906 Association Drive
Reston, VA 22091
(703) 860-5317
Douglas W. Hunt, Chairman

This nonprofit organization is committed to establishing standards for educational travel and exchange programs and monitoring for compliance with those standards on behalf of schools, educational groups, and communities. Standards are established both for programs in which U.S. students go abroad and those in which foreign students come to the United States.

PUBLICATIONS: The Council on Standards for International Educational Travel publishes an annual *Advisory List of International Educational Travel Exchange Programs.* The list describes more than 30 international exchange programs that meet the standards established by the Council. The list is designed for use by parents, teachers, and prospective exchange students.

Educational Foundation for Foreign Study
1528 Chapala Street
Santa Barbara, CA 93101
(805) 963-0553
Fran Radford, Program Coordinator

This public foundation provides homestay and study programs for U.S. teenagers abroad as well as teenagers from more than 19 countries who wish to come to the United States. Program options include semester-long and year-long programs, as well as a special scholarship program for creative U.S. students from disadvantaged backgrounds.

PUBLICATIONS: None.

Educators for Social Responsibility (ESR)
23 Garden Street
Cambridge, MA 02138
(617) 492-1764
Susan Alexander, Executive Director

ESR is a membership organization open to individuals committed to developing new ways of addressing conflict and diversity in a nuclear age. Educational objectives of the organization focus on teaching students to think rationally and creatively about public policy issues with international dimensions; developing student ability to recognize and adopt a range of perspectives in analyzing issues; fostering within students decision-making and citizenship participation skills; and helping students develop a vision of the future.

ESR offers the following services nationwide: teacher training programs; development and publication of curriculum materials for adult and student audiences; local conferences in the Boston area; a speakers bureau; local and state chapter activities, and a reference collection on nuclear education issues.

PUBLICATIONS: ESR has a number of curriculum and resource guides available. Sample titles are *Taking Part; Investigations: Toxic Waste; Perspectives: A Teaching Guide To Concepts of Peace; Getting Acquainted: Thinking About the Soviet Union;* and *Decision Making in a Nuclear Age. Forum,* a quarterly newsletter, is available to members.

ERIC Clearinghouse for Social Studies/Social Science Education (ERIC/ChESS)
2805 East 10th Street
Bloomington, IN 47405
(812) 335-3838
John Patrick, Director

One of the subject-specialized clearinghouses in the national Educational Resources Information Center (ERIC) system, ERIC/ChESS reviews, selects, and annotates social studies and social science education materials for the ERIC database. In addition, ERIC/ChESS provides information services for social studies educators including computer searches of the ERIC database, annotated bibliographies, and brief state-of-the-art reports on selected topics.

PUBLICATIONS: ERIC/ChESS publishes a free biannual newsletter, *Keeping Up,* and low-cost resource materials. Titles pertaining to global and international education include *Teaching About Japan; Teaching About the Pacific Rim; The African Social Studies Programme: An Effort to Improve Curriculum and Instruction Across 17 African Nations;* and *Global Resources.*

The Experiment in International Living
Kipling Road
Brattleboro, VT 05301
(802) 257-7751
Alan Carter, Vice President for International Programs

The Experiment in International Living promotes international
understanding through exchange programs including study-abroad programs
for high school, college, and professional students; undergraduate and
graduate programs in intercultural management; language teacher training;
and overseas refugee and community development training programs.
Programs for American teachers and students include student exchange and
study abroad; B.A. and M.A. degree programs; an annual global education
summer institute; and consultation services in cross-cultural, global, and
developmental education.

PUBLICATIONS: The Experiment in International Living publishes a free
quarterly magazine, *Odyssey,* as well as a range of student- and teacher-
focused publications.

Foreign Policy Association (FPA)
205 Lexington Avenue
New York, NY 10016
(212) 481-8450
Mary E. Soley, Director of School Programs

The Foreign Policy Association (FPA) is a national, nonprofit organization
dedicated to world affairs education at all levels. The Association's
publications and programs offer nonpartisan background information and a
forum for discussion on significant foreign policy issues facing the United
States and the world. The Department of School Programs sponsors student-
and teacher-focused publications, curriculum materials, teacher workshops,
and student institutes.

PUBLICATIONS: FPA publications particularly relevant to precollege
programs in international education include *Great Decisions,* an annual
publication that analyzes eight major contemporary foreign policy issues;
*Guide to Careers in World Affairs; America in the World: A Guide to U.S.
Foreign Policy;* and *Teacher's Resource Guide: Lessons on Current U.S. Foreign
Policy Issues for Secondary Social Studies Courses.*

Global Education Associates
475 Riverside Drive
Suite 456
New York, NY 10115
(201) 870-3290
Patricia and Gerald Mische, Founders

Global Education Associates conducts research, curriculum development, and training programs for educator groups. Specific services include consultation to school districts, workshops on global issues and topics, and materials development and dissemination. Topics of specific interest to the organization are teaching about global issues through community linkages, hunger, human rights, and the environment. Membership is available for an annual fee, which includes subscription to a newsletter and a monograph series.

PUBLICATIONS: Global Education Associates publishes the *Associates Newsletter* for members; *The Whole Earth Papers,* a monograph series; and *Toward a Human World Order.*

Global Education Center
College of Education
University of Minnesota
110 Pattee Hall
150 Pillsbury Drive, SE
Minneapolis, MN 55455
(612) 386-4580
John J. Cogan, Director

A special program of the University of Minnesota College of Education, the Global Education Center provides services to university faculty, students, and teachers concerned with global education. Services are aimed primarily at Minnesota educational audiences but are also delivered throughout the Midwest. These services include conferences, educational workshops, consultation to educators and school districts on curriculum and program development, exchange and study abroad information, and overseas travel opportunities. The program is funded to conduct regional studies development and travel programs for educators with Japan, the People's Republic of China, and Western Europe.

PUBLICATIONS: The Global Education Center offers a free newsletter as well as occasional papers and bibliographies.

Global Education Motivators (GEM)
Montgomery County Intermediate Unit Building
Paper Mill Road and Montgomery Avenue
Erdenheim, PA 19118
(215) 233-9558
Robert Schell, Director

Global Education Motivators (GEM) is a national organization to promote global education in elementary and secondary schools as well as the community through curriculum programs, teacher training, and study/travel programs. GEMRIM is the corporation's program for global education curriculum development in K-12 education, GEMQUEST is the study/travel program, and GEMGRAM is the teacher workshop program. Through GEMNET, GEM offers U.S. classrooms the opportunity to link with classrooms in other nations.

PUBLICATIONS: A newsletter describing GEM's programs is available.

Global Learning
40 South Fullerton Avenue
Montclair, NJ 07042
(201) 783-7616
Jeffrey Brown, Executive Director

Global Learning promotes global education in elementary and secondary schools through a variety of projects aimed at teacher, administrator, teacher trainer, parent, and community audiences. Services include program presentations, teacher training and inservice programs, curriculum development workshops, and credit-bearing courses in cooperation with local colleges. Topics of special interest in the organization's training and curriculum development activities are food/hunger/developing nations, conflict resolution, environment, and multicultural studies.

PUBLICATIONS: The program produces a variety of free and low-cost resource materials, including a quarterly newsletter of global education materials and training opportunities, *Gleanings; Global Learning Teacher Education Manual;* and bibliographies and resource lists on selected global education topics. *Coalition Building for Global Perspectives: A Process and Resource Manual,* a guide to developing sound, community-supported global education programs, is available free through Global Learning.

The Hunger Project
1388 Sutter Street
San Francisco, CA 94109
(415) 928-8700
Kathleen Kook, Director of Education

The Hunger Project seeks to raise awareness worldwide of the problem of hunger and the issues involved in ending hunger. To contribute to the elimination of world hunger by the end of the twentieth century, the Project sponsors educational programs and publications. Sample services include a teacher inservice program on ending hunger, teacher training, youth and student clubs, and a national volunteer network.

PUBLICATIONS: The Project regularly publishes a newspaper, *A Shift in the Wind,* as well as occasional papers and a newsletter, *World Development Forum.* It also offers two audiovisual programs, *Africa: The Possibility* and *InterAction.* A book, *Ending Hunger: An Idea Whose Time Has Come,* discusses the problem of hunger, areas of the world in serious trouble from hunger, and strategies and solutions.

Immaculate Heart College Center
10951 West Pico Boulevard, #2021
Los Angeles, CA 90064
(213) 470-2293
Margaret-Rose Welch, Director

The focus of the Immaculate Heart College Center is to encourage and
facilitate effective educational programs related to peace and global
cooperation through an emphasis on human rights, universal human values,
international communications, and conflict resolution. Services include
community awareness programs on conflict areas of the world, teacher
training, consultation to school districts, and development and dissemination
of curriculum materials and teacher resources. Services of the Center are
limited primarily to California and the Southwest.

PUBLICATIONS: The Center produces a bimonthly newsletter, *Global
Pages,* which cites resources and events of interest to teachers. The Center
also makes available a video series, *Human Values in a Nuclear Age,* and a
slide show, *Address: Earth.*

Information Center on Children's Cultures
United States Committee for UNICEF
331 East 38th Street
New York, NY 10016
(212) 686-5522
Janet Smith, Librarian

The Information Center on Children's Cultures collects educational and
cultural materials about children around the world that are appropriate for
use by children from pre-kindergarten through middle school age. The
Center's collection includes books, audiovisual materials, and periodicals,
among other works. Special topics within the collection are Third World
area studies, cross-cultural communication, ethnic studies, food and hunger,
multicultural education, and development education. Special services of the
Center include developing and disseminating bibliographies, conducting
workshop services for teachers, and maintaining a research library.

PUBLICATIONS: The Center offers a wide variety of materials including
a free kit titled *Childhood Problems Worldwide: Nutrition and Safe Water,*
a slide show on the same topic; and free kits on Ecuador, Ghana, Sri Lanka,
Senegal, and Thailand.

**International Society for Intercultural Education, Training, and Research
(SIETAR International)**
1505 Twenty-second Street, NW
Washington, DC 20037
(202) 296-4710
Diane Zeller, Executive Director

SIETAR International is an international membership organization of professionals in the fields of cross-cultural communication and research. Members come from higher and precollegiate education, government, business and industry, and cultural organizations. Membership fees range from $2,000 for lifetime membership to $25/year for student membership. SIETAR's goal is to raise awareness of the cross-cultural imperative inherent in our increasingly global society and to contribute to the solution of global problems. The organization sponsors an annual conference, a summer institute and workshop program, and professional referrals.

PUBLICATIONS: An extensive publications program focuses on cross-cultural communication strategies. Sample titles include *Cross-Cultural Encounters: Face to Face Interactions* and *Training for the Cross-Cultural Mind.*

Las Palomas de Taos
Box 3400
Taos, NM 87571
(505) 758-9456
George Otero, Director

Las Palomas de Taos sponsors a variety of multicultural, cross-cultural, and global education programs for teachers and students. A workshop series is offered each year on special topics. Additionally, schools or educator groups may work with the Center to develop a program for special audiences. The Center is available for extended retreats for student and adult groups. Staff work with school districts and other programs to develop curriculum and programs. Located in the culturally rich and diverse area of northern New Mexico, the center utilizes its immediate environment in emphasizing respect for diversity as a global imperative.

PUBLICATIONS: Two resource books are available from the center: *Handbook of Successful Elements of Inservice Training in Global Education* and *Handbook for Developing School Improvement Networks in Global Education.*

Mershon Center
The Ohio State University
199 West 10th Street
Columbus, OH 43201
(614) 422-1681
Richard C. Remy, Director

The Mershon Center, an endowed social science education center within the university, conducts two special programs related to global education: Citizenship Development and Global Education, and the Consortium for International Studies Education. Through support from government and private foundations grants, the Center conducts research, provides teacher training, and develops curriculum materials on the topics of foreign policy, national security in a global age, international relations, world history, and community-global linkages. Center services are available to school districts, institutes of higher education, community groups, and government agencies.

PUBLICATIONS: The Mershon Center offers a variety of curriculum materials developed through Center-conducted projects. These include a series entitled *Bringing a Global Perspective,* which offers separate curriculum volumes for infusing global studies into secondary-level American history, economics, world history, and geography courses; *World Regions: The Local Connection*; and a series on teaching national security issues in secondary-level American history, American government, world history, economics, and geography courses. A Center newsletter is available free of charge.

National Council for the Social Studies (NCSS)
3501 Newark Street, NW
Washington, DC 20016
(202) 966-7840
Fran Haley, Executive Director

A national membership organization for social studies educators at all levels, NCSS works to promote social studies education for responsible citizenship. In addition to offering publications and conferences, NCSS, through special committees, develops and encourages policy and practice related to educational research, teacher training and professional development, curriculum development, and innovative practices. NCSS also offers support to social studies educators and provides professional growth opportunities through travel-study programs, workshops, and seminars. A standing committee of NCSS and several special interest groups focus on teaching international relations and area studies.

PUBLICATIONS: In addition to a newsletter and journal distributed to the membership, NCSS publishes several bulletins on selected social studies topics each year. Bulletin topics related to global education and international studies include *Canada in the Classroom*; *Teaching of World History*; *Teaching Social Studies in Other Nations*; *International Human Rights, Society, and the Schools*; and *Perspectives on Japan: A Guide for Teachers.*

National Council of World Affairs Organizations
Third Floor, Wanamaker Building
1300 Market Street
Philadelphia, PA 19107
(215) 563-5363
Mrs. Buntzie Ellis Churchill, Jr., President

The National Council of World Affairs Organizations is the central association of more than 40 local world affairs councils around the United States. The Council works to improve the work of its local member organizations. Additionally, it offers resource materials for study and discussion, and strives to develop awareness among the general public of important public policy issues related to world affairs.

PUBLICATIONS: None.

Office on Global Education
Church World Service, NCCC USA
2115 North Charles Street
Baltimore, MD 21218
(301) 727-6106
Susan Soohoo, Administrative Assistant

The Office on Global Education works nationally to inform and sensitize the U.S. public about the causes and issues surrounding hunger, limited global resources, economic development, and global interdependence. The Office seeks to support and collaborate with existing programs in global education. Services include educational consultation and collaboration, networking, research and development, and materials development.

PUBLICATIONS: The Office on Global Education has published a World Food Day curriculum and a global calendar. Additionally, it offers fact sheets on global issues such as hunger and development and a global issues reprint series.

The Ohio State University, College of Education
223 Arps Hall
1945 North High Street
Columbus, OH 43210
(614) 422-5381
M. Eugene Gilliom, Professor of Social Studies Education

The Ohio State University College of Education undertakes a variety of activities and projects to further international education. These include study-tour programs to Asia, Africa, and the Soviet Union, available to educators nationwide; student teaching opportunities abroad for language and social studies teachers; and graduate courses in global education.

PUBLICATIONS: The College of Education produces a newsletter for the Committee for International Tele-education.

Open Door Student Exchange
124 East Merrick Road
P.O. Box 1150
Valley Stream, NY 11582
(516) 825-8485
Howard Bertenthal, President

This organization provides opportunities for high school students from more than 25 countries to live with families and attend schools abroad. Several options are available, including three-month, six-month, and one-year study programs. Special art seminars in Europe and foreign correspondent programs in Latin America are available for U.S. students.
PUBLICATIONS: None.

People-to-People International
2420 Pershing Road, Suite 300
Kansas City, MO 64108
(816) 421-6343
Thomas Stillitano, Jr., Chief Executive Officer

People-to-People International is a nonpolitical, nonprofit, volunteer organization that operates both nationally and through more than 75 local U.S. chapters and more than 25 international chapters. The organization seeks to promote increased international understanding through the establishment of personal relationships between Americans and people throughout the world. People-to-People sponsors adult and student travel and exchange programs, homestays for international visitors, pen-pal programs, and international classroom exchanges.
PUBLICATIONS: People-to-People publishes a quarterly newsletter of activities entitled *People.* Brochures describing the organization's programs and services are also available.

Population Reference Bureau
777 14th Street, NW
Suite 800
Washington, DC 20005
(202) 639-8040
Carey Davis, Administrative Director

The Population Reference Bureau is a nonprofit educational organization established in 1929. The Bureau is a source of information on the facts and implications of national and world population trends.
PUBLICATIONS: The Population Reference Bureau publishes a quarterly newsletter during the academic year as well as population data sheets and short reports.

Sister Cities International
1625 Eye Street, NE
Suites 424–426
Washington, DC 20006
(202) 293-5504
Thomas Gittins, Executive Vice President

This nonprofit organization seeks to promote better international cooperation and understanding by creating sister-city affiliations between U.S. cities and cities around the world. Sister Cities International serves as a center for research, information, and counseling for U.S. communities interested in establishing or maintaining such a relationship.
PUBLICATIONS: None.

Social Science Education Consortium, Inc. (SSEC)
855 Broadway
Boulder, CO 80302
(303) 492-8154
James Giese, Executive Director

A national nonprofit organization, SSEC undertakes projects to improve the teaching of social studies at all grade levels, K–12. SSEC offers consultation and program planning services to school districts throughout the United States and offers a number of publications on global education topics. SSEC conducts special projects in Asian area studies and international educational exchange.

PUBLICATIONS: A global issues series includes *Global Issues: Activities and Resources for High School Teachers*; *Global Issues: Activities and Resources for the Middle School*; and *Global Issues: Elementary Activities*. Additional titles on global and international themes are *Japan in the Classroom: Elementary and Secondary Activities*; *Teaching About Korea*; *Teaching About Peace and Nuclear War: A Balanced Approach*; and *Teaching About the Future*.

Social Studies Development Center
Indiana University
2805 East 10th Street
Bloomington, IN 47405
(812) 335-3838
John Patrick, Director

The Social Studies Development Center of the Indiana University School of Education undertakes research, curriculum development, and teacher training programs related to all aspects of the K–12 social studies curriculum. The Center has conducted a number of projects related to global education and international studies, including "Indiana and the World" and "The Midwest and the World"; "Internationalizing Teacher Education"; and the "Midwest Program for Teaching About Japan." Through its operation of the ERIC Clearinghouse for Social Studies/Social Science Education, the Social Studies Development Center offers reference lists and computer searches, as well as several publications on global education.

PUBLICATIONS: No publications separate from ERIC/ChESS.

Stanford Program on International and Cross-Cultural Education (SPICE)
Littlefield Center
Room 14
Stanford University
Stanford, CA 94305-5013
(415) 723-1114
Judith Wooster, Director

The Stanford Program on International and Cross-Cultural Education (SPICE) is a long-term effort for international and cross-cultural education in elementary and secondary schools. The Program provides teacher training and curriculum development in the areas of international studies, world cultures, and global issues. The Program has ongoing projects in China studies, Japan studies, conflict resolution, and Latin America studies.

PUBLICATIONS: SPICE conducts an extensive publications program, devoted predominantly to curriculum guides and activity books for the elementary and secondary social studies and foreign language classroom. Sample titles include *China Resources: A Guide for the Classroom; Demystifying the Chinese Language; Teaching About a Changing China; Nuclear Arms Education in Secondary Schools; Castletowns: An Introduction to Tokugawa, Japan; Introduction to International Trade;* and *Japan Meets the West: A Case Study of Perceptions.*

The Stanley Foundation, Cooperative Projects in International Education
420 East Third Street
Muscatine, IA 52761
(319) 264-1500
Jan Drum, Project Coordinator

The Stanley Foundation sponsors a range of projects for schools, churches, business groups, and other organizations. Programs and projects are developed to meet the specific needs of the audience group. Sample programs have focused on global perspectives in education, U.S.-Soviet relations, conflict resolution, and international resource development and management. Services offered by the Cooperative Projects include consultation, teacher and staff workshops, presentations, and resource networking.

PUBLICATIONS: The Stanley Foundation offers a variety of conference reports, occasional papers, and audiocassettes on international issues.

The Foundation also publishes *World Press Review,* a monthly magazine containing reprints of articles published outside the United States.

United States Information Agency (USIA)
301 4th Street, SW
Washington, DC 20547
(202) 485-2355

The United States Information Agency (USIA) operates a vast number of programs related to international exchange. Of special interest to precollegiate education are the Teacher Exchange Programs and Group Projects Abroad Program of the Fulbright-Hays Program. USIA also coordinates the International Youth Exchange Program, which awards grants to U.S. private groups to enable them to conduct exchanges of high-school-age students.

PUBLICATIONS: Each section of USIA conducts its own publications program.

World Affairs Council of Philadelphia
John Wanamaker Building
1300 Market Street
Philadelphia, PA 19107
(215) 922-2900
Margaret Lonzetta, Director of Student/Teachers Activities

Funded by grants from public and private sources, the World Affairs Council of Philadelphia is a nonprofit, nonpartisan organization dedicated to increasing the awareness of international affairs throughout the Delaware Valley. The Council provides a wide range of programs, including forums and seminars for corporate executives, professionals, and individuals, as well as educational enrichment for teachers and students on the topic of world affairs. The Council works with the School District of Philadelphia to maintain an international studies magnet high school. It also sponsors a model United Nations program for high school students.

PUBLICATIONS: The Council produces a newsletter as well as short curriculum publications for educators and a variety of resources for the community.

The World Bank
1818 H Street, NW
Washington, DC 20433
(202) 477-1234
William A. Branigan, Public Information

The World Bank is an international institution owned by 151 countries. Its mission is to assist its developing member countries in improving the living conditions of their people. To this end, the World Bank lends money for development projects and for structural and sectoral adjustment and also offers various types of technical assistance.

PUBLICATIONS: The World Bank has an extensive educational publications program including books, multimedia materials, videocassettes, and poster kits. All focus on development education and international development issues.

Youth For Understanding (YFU)
3501 Newark Street, NW
Washington, DC 20016-3167
(800) USA-0200
Jody Olson, Vice President, Programs

Youth For Understanding (YFU) is a private, nonprofit organization that arranges international exchanges for secondary students. There are several programs, including international students in the United States; U.S. students overseas; the Japan-U.S. Senate Scholarship Program, which enables two U.S. students from each state to study in Japan on a full scholarship summer program; the Congress-Bundestag Youth Exchange, providing full scholarships for year-abroad programs to U.S. and German youth; and the Finland-U.S. Senate Youth Exchange Program, funded by the Finnish government to enable U.S. students to spend the summer in Finland.

PUBLICATIONS: YFU publishes orientation materials for students involved in its international exchanges, including *Introduction to Japan: A Workbook.*

Reference Works

6

General Reference Works

Editorials on File.
New York: Facts on File. 1970 to present.
Number of pages varies. 1970–1984 complete set of microfiche: $435.
Subsequent volumes will become available on microfiche every two years.

The archive of *Editorials on File* contains more than 45,000 full-text editorials selected from leading U.S. and Canadian newspapers. Indexes will help students locate editorials related to international relations and issues.

Kaleidoscope: Current World Data.
Santa Barbara, CA: ABC-CLIO, 1984 to present.
One-year subscription: $495, with discounts available for schools and libraries. (There is a one-time UPS shipping fee of $55 on new orders, plus $25 bulk rate postage and handling for 52 supplements; for optional first-class postage/ handling add $79.)

This reference tool comes in the form of a compact datacard file containing a section on more than 180 countries of the world, plus all the major international organizations and special interest sections. The file is kept up to date with weekly card supplements and news summaries. Each country file contains (1) a General Data and Government section, which includes a map, demographic information, vital statistics, financial figures, military information, government structure and officials, and other vital data; and (2) a Chronological File, which includes an extensive chronology of major economic, social, military, and political events. The file contains over 4,200 datacards with tab dividers, and subscribers receive a tabletop file cabinet, a videocassette user aid, and a periodic newsletter.

Annual Editions

Annual Editions: Global Issues 87/88. 3d ed.
Guilford, CT: Dushkin Publishing Group, 1987.
256p. $9.50. ISBN 0-87967-684-1.

Published annually, this book contains a collection of readings on selected topics including natural resources, development, conflict, communication, and human values. A topic guide, unit overviews, and challenge questions are included. An instructor's resource guide is available.

Annual Editions: World Politics 87/88. 8th ed.
Guilford, CT: Dushkin Publishing Group, 1987.
288p. $9.50. ISBN 0-87967-689-2.

More than 48 reading selections treat the topics of the United States as a world power, U.S. allies, the Third World, the international political economy, the arms race, and international law. A glossary, topic guide, unit overviews, and challenge questions are included.

Current Issues: Critical Issues Confronting the Nation and the World.
Arlington, VA: Close Up Foundation, 1986–
245p. $8 each or $6 with an order for 21 or more, plus a free teacher's guide. ISBN 0-932765-01-7.

Intended for use with high school students, this annual publication contains background readings on domestic and foreign policy issues. Several chapters in the 1986 edition will be of interest to students of international affairs, energy, environment, defense, international trade, world poverty, and U.S. foreign aid. Televised seminars based on these readings are available through Close Up Video Services.

Facts on File Yearbooks.
New York: Facts on File, 1941–
Number of pages varies. $85/volume.

Since 1941, *Facts on File* has summarized, recorded, and indexed the news of the nation and the world. Published at the end of each year, each volume contains all of the year's 52 weekly news digests and an annual index that will allow students to pinpoint information on international news stories.

Great Decisions.
Moepli, Nancy L., ed. New York: Foreign Policy Association, 1987.
Approximately 96p. $6. ISBN 0-87124-114-5.

Each year, this annual publication for community and classroom use focuses on eight major international issues. Each article identifies vital points for discussion of U.S. foreign policy. Suggested additional readings are cited. The *Great Decisions Teacher's Guide* is available separately.

Information Please Almanac '87.
Boston: Houghton Mifflin, 1986.
1,007p. $5.95. ISBN 6-88615.

This quick reference is an excellent source of information on international population data, including current events, world records, heads of government, and so on.

State of the World 1988: A Worldwatch Institute Report on Progress Toward a Sustainable Society.
Brown, Lester, ed. New York: Norton, 1988.
263p. $9.95. ISBN 0-393-02515-2.

The articles in the 1988 edition of this annual publication examine the state of the earth, energy futures, raising energy efficiency, renewable energy sources, reforestation, extinction of species, toxic chemicals, the Strategic Defense Initiative, and the global family.

Atlases

Atlas of the Third World.
George Thomas Kurian. New York: Facts on File, 1982.
382p. $95. ISBN 0-87196-673-5.

More than 1,000 maps and charts examine the Third World as a cultural, geographic, political, and economic area and as a composite of individual countries.

Atlas of United States Foreign Relations.
Washington, DC: Superintendent of Documents, U.S. Government Printing Office, 1983.
96p. $5. ISBN 0-318-19995.

Basic information about U.S. foreign relations if provided, including information about international organizations, elements of the world economy, trade and investment, development assistance, and U.S. national security.

Contemporary World Atlas.
Culver City, CA: Social Studies School Service (distributor), 1984.
256p. $8.95.

This atlas gives a continent-by-continent overview that includes information on economics, geography, and climate. Special topic maps on population are provided. The atlas also includes nine pages of detailed maps of each nation and individual U.S. states.

GAIA: An Atlas of Planet Management.
Norman Myers. Garden City, NY: Anchor Press, 1984.
256p. $17.95. ISBN 0-385-19072-7.

Seven sections deal with the interaction of humankind and the environment. Topics and issues such as land, ocean, and evolution are presented from the perspective of resource management.

Global Perspectives Maps.
Wellesley, MA: World Eagle, 1983.
$3.95, individual maps; $20–$29, sets.

Originally published by the *Christian Science Monitor,* ten maps present the following perspectives: the United States as seen from Canada, Africa as seen from India, East Europe as seen from West Europe, Southeast Asia as seen from the People's Republic of China, North Africa as seen from the Mideast, China as seen from Japan, Central Africa as seen from South Africa, Latin America as seen from Cuba, the Mideast as seen from Israel. The maps are available in folded or laminated versions for classroom use.

Goode's World Atlas, 17th ed.
Chicago: Rand McNally, 1986.
367p. $19.95. ISBN 528-63006-7.

Covered are major physical-cultural and socioeconomic aspects of the world in maps, graphs, and tabular materials. This atlas is an excellent source of economic information.

The Great World Atlas.
Maplewood, NJ: Hammond, 1986.
351p. $39.95.

More than 125 maps detail every region of the world and provide global comparisons of topics such as population, language, resources, trade, education, climate, nutrition, and energy. Traditional maps are supplemented by 20 full-color satellite maps.

Maps on File.
New York: Facts on File, 1986.
$145. Annual update: $35. ISBN 0-8160-1287-3.

More than 400 reproducible maps in two volumes covering every country of the world, oceans, continents, and major economic and political issues in contemporary world affairs.

The New State of the World Atlas.
Michael Kidron and Ronald Segal. New York: Simon and Schuster, 1987.
57 maps. $9.95. ISBN 0-671-42438-4.

Containing world maps that identify major topics of public concern, this atlas can be used with students in grades 7–12. A section of the atlas contains a discussion of each map. Of special interest are the sections on (1) Natural Resources—maps dealing with the world mineral power, energy power, oil power, nuclear power, and food power; (2) the Economy—maps showing industrial power, technological power, dependence and diversity, trade power, national income, the debt-laden South, and margins of safety; (3) Business—maps showing national money reserves, national income, and the nationality of transnationals; and (4) Labor—maps showing exploitation, the labor force, and women workers. The Center for Teaching International Relations (University of Denver, Denver, CO 80208) sells a publication that can be used to supplement the atlas. It sells for $21.95 and includes reproducible student handout/exercise sheets.

Oxford Economic Atlas of the World, 4th ed.
London: Oxford University Press, 1972.
239p. $14.95.

There are two main parts to this atlas: (1) world maps grouped by subjects (e.g., environment, crops, livestock, energy, manufacturing, industry, demography), and (2) a statistical supplement arranged alphabetically by country. Most maps in the atlas are based on the period 1963–1965. Comparative figures are for the period 1953–1955.

The State of the World Maps.
London: Pictorial Charts Educational Trust, 1986.
7 wall maps. $15.75.

Seven theme maps from *The New State of the World Atlas* have been enlarged as visual aids for classroom use. Maps range in size from 13½" × 20" to 20" × 30". Each map comes with background notes and activity suggestions. Map themes include the proliferation of nations since World War II; strategic nuclear balance; ongoing conflicts; dietary differences; variations in life expectancy; methods of national rule; and dominant religion by country.

Strategic Atlas: Comparative Geopolitics of the World's Powers.
Gerald Chali and Jean-Pierre Rageau. New York: Harper and Row, 1985. *224p. $14.95. ISBN 0-06-091220-0.*

This specialized atlas conveys in map format the social, military, and industrial components of national power and illustrates how power is distributed around the world. Sample topics conveyed through maps are raw materials, industrial resources, balance of strategic military weapons, gross national product, and demographic data.

Today Series.
Wellesley, MA: World Eagle, 1984.
150–160p. Variable prices.

This series of atlas publications includes three volumes: *Africa Today: An Atlas of Reproducible Pages; Europe Today: An Atlas of Reproducible Pages;* and *Latin America Today: An Atlas of Reproducible Pages.* Each volume contains maps, tables, and graphs for all the countries of the given world area. Map topics are size, population, resources, commodities, trade, religion, cities, food and agriculture, health, schooling, jobs, energy, and demographic statistics. Individual country maps are also provided.

The Whole Earth Atlas.
Maplewood, NJ: Hammond, 1986.
256p. $8.95.

Through maps and accompanying data, this atlas details contemporary, changing world events. In addition to traditional political maps of the countries of the world, it includes color maps depicting agriculture, industry, resources, languages, and religion.

The World Atlas of Revolution.
Andrew Wheatcroft. New York: Simon and Schuster, 1983.
208p. $6.95. ISBN 0-671-47207-0.

This publication examines revolutions—their causes, successes, and failures—through maps, photographs, and text. The atlas covers revolutions around the world from 1765 through the 1980s.

The World Bank Atlas.
Washington, DC: The World Bank, 1987.
32p. $6.50. ISBN 0-686-39723-1.

This color atlas contains tables, charts, and maps with data for more than 180 countries and territories. Sample data include gross national product (GNP), population, population growth rate, GNP per capita, life expectancy at birth, total fertility rate, and school enrollment ratio. The text is presented in three languages: English, French, and Spanish.

Bibliographies

Bibliography of Nuclear Age Educational Resources.
Stanford, CA: Stanford Program on International and Cross-Cultural Education, 1987.
111p. $15.95.

This annotated bibliography includes kindergarten through adult curriculum materials, texts and reference books, articles, and other bibliographies on security and conflict issues and nuclear-age education. For each entry, advocacy positions, grade level, and availability are noted.

"Defining Global Education: A Resource List."
Jaimie P. Cloud and Lynn Parisi. *Social Education* 50 no. 6 (October 1986): 448–452.

This annotated listing describes selected teacher and classroom resources on global education. Commercial materials, ERIC resources, and project-developed materials are included under the headings Human Values, Global Systems, Global Issues and Problems, and Global History.

Free and Inexpensive Materials on World Affairs.
Leonard S. Kenworthy. Kennett Square, PA: World Affairs Materials, 1983.
92p. $5 plus postage.

This bibliography lists more than 2,500 resource materials under $2. Many are free. Cited materials focus on world issues, regions of the world, individual countries, the United Nations, and so on. Many of the materials, such as maps, posters, kits, and films, are of special interest to educators.

Global Education.
Culver City, CA: Social Studies School Service, 1988.
80p. Updated annually. Free.

This bibliography annotates commercially published K–12 classroom materials on global education, which are distributed by the Social Studies

School Service. A wide variety of print, audiovisual, and computer software materials are included under the topic headings Issues; Cold War/U.S.-Soviet Relations; Cross-Cultural Studies; Geography; Terrorism/World Ideologies; U.S. Foreign Policy; Vietnam; and War and Peace Issues. For each entry, price and publisher are noted.

The Global Resource Book.
New York: Global Perspectives in Education, Inc., 1986.
293p. $50 with binder, $45 without binder.

Resources, including background materials, curriculum materials, and audiovisual materials related to global/international topics, are cited. Topics treated range from global economics, development, environment, peace/war, and U.S. foreign policy to various area studies regions. The book comes in a looseleaf format to facilitate revisions and additions of listings offered periodically by the publisher.

Global Resources.
James Becker and Deborah Hutton. Bloomington, IN: ERIC Clearinghouse for Social Studies/Social Science Education, 1988.
25p. $1.

This annotated bibliography of global education resources for K–12 teachers and students is divided into sections on professional organizations, foundations and special projects, journals and newsletters, Educational Resources Information Center (ERIC) resources, journal articles, commercial materials, teacher resources, computer software, simulations and games, and reports.

The New Global Yellow Pages.
New York: Global Perspectives in Education, 1986.
170p. $30.

This bibliography provides annotated listings of organizations and projects around the United States that are involved in global and international education. For each organization, activities, contact people, and publications are cited.

Resources for Teaching About Global Economics.
New York: Global Perspectives in Education, 1985.
5p. $2.

Described in this bibliography are resources that secondary school teachers can use to teach about global economics, including classroom materials and library reference resources.

Encyclopedias

Encyclopaedia Britannica, 16th ed.
Chicago: Encyclopaedia Britannica Educational Corporation, 1987.
$1,049 (includes free rolling book cart). ISBN 0-85229-444-1.

The *Encyclopaedia Britannica* is a good encyclopedia to use for broad
summaries of economics and economics-related topics. Useful for high
school students.

Encyclopedia Americana.
Danbury, CT: Grolier, 1987.
$799 plus $23 shipping.

The *Encyclopedia Americana* is an excellent source of information,
containing broad summaries on the countries of the world and enduring
international issues. Useful for middle school and high school students.

Encyclopedia of the Third World.
New York: Facts on File, 1983.
2,384p. 3-volume set, $175. ISBN 0-8160-1118-4.

The Third World constitutes more than half the population and two-thirds
of the nations of the world. This encyclopedia contains entries on all the
nations of the Third World, including data on ethnicity, economics, standard
of living, government, religion, and so on.

The Facts on File Dictionary of Human Geography.
Brian Goodall. New York: Facts on File, 1987.
528p. $24.95. ISBN 0-8160-1738-7.

Designed for college students, this dictionary may also be useful to
secondary students. It includes all terms currently used by human
geographers to describe geographic concepts, people/environmental
relationships, geographic planning, and quantitative techniques.

World Education Encyclopedia.
George Kurian. New York: Facts on File, 1987.
1,440p. 3 volumes, $145. ISBN 0-87196-748-0.

This encyclopedia provides an overview of the history and current state of
education for nearly every country of the world. The encyclopedia is divided
into sections on global education statistics, country entries, international
educational rankings, and international educational organizations and
affiliations.

The World Encyclopedia of Political Systems and Parties.
New York: Facts on File, 1987.
2 volumes, $179. ISBN 0-8160-1539-2.

Contains articles by more than 100 political scientists and academic experts describing the branches of each nation's government, as well as leadership, structural organization, history, constituency, and financing.

The Worldmark Encyclopedia of the Nations, 6th ed.
Moshe Sachs, ed. New York: John Wiley and Sons, 1984.
1,800p. $225. ISBN 0-471-88622.

The purpose of this encyclopedia is to provide a "portrait of the world." Provided are descriptions of 172 countries. Fifty different subjects, clearly defined in bold print, are examined for each country.

Handbooks

Background Notes on the Countries of the World.
Washington, DC: Superintendent of Documents, U.S. Government Printing Office. Dates vary.
Number of pages varies. $34.

This is a series of short, factual pamphlets about the various countries and territories of the world. Each pamphlet contains information on the country's land, people, history, government, political conditions, economy, and foreign relations.

Culturegram (series).
Provo, UT: Brigham Young University. Dates vary.
4p. $.35 each.

Handy summaries are provided for approximately 80 countries. Each *Culturegram* details geography, population, social customs, history, and other special characteristics, and is three-hole punched for easy binding. A complete set of the *Culturegram* series is also available. Materials are updated periodically.

Economic Handbook of the World.
Arthur S. Banks. New York: McGraw-Hill, 1982.
608p. $39.96. ISBN 0-07-003692-6.

This is the first in a new series of annual world economic surveys. It contains current macro- and microeconomic data for all countries, regions, international organizations, and multinational corporations. Comprehensive in scope, this handbook includes expert analyses of current situations.

Foreign Area Studies (Area Handbook Series).
Washington, DC: Superintendent of Documents, U.S. Government Printing Office. Dates vary.
Number of pages varies. Price falls within $12–$13 range.

Part of the Department of the Army's *Area Handbook Series,* these books describe and analyze the economic, military, political, and social systems and institutions of a particular foreign country. Origins and traditions of the people and social and national attitudes are also discussed.

Global Guide to International Education.
David S. Hoopes. New York: Facts on File, 1984.
704p. $95. ISBN 0-87196-437-6.

A thorough and authoritative source on global and international education programs. Separate sections cover general information sources, curriculum resources, educational exchange organizations, international studies programs, peace and conflict resolution studies, professional education, grants and awards, study abroad, foreign language, publishers, and area studies programs.

Handbook of the Nations, 6th ed.
Detroit: Gale Research, 1986.
274p. $78. ISBN 0-8103-1590-4.

Up-to-date economic and governmental data are provided for 191 nations. Details concerning each nation's land, people, communications, and defense forces are included.

Handbooks to the World Series.
New York: Facts on File, 1986.
> **Western Europe.**
> Richard Mayne, ed.
> *600p. $40. ISBN 0-8160-1261-X.*
> **The Soviet Union and Eastern Europe.**
> George Schopflin, ed.
> *600p. $40. ISBN 0-8160-1260-1.*

Each volume of this series contains the latest comparative statistics, in tabular form, covering all of the countries in the area. Major sections dealing with the economics of the countries are provided, as well as background articles.

The New Book of World Rankings.
George Kurian. New York: Facts on File, 1983.
448p. $29.95. ISBN 0-87196-743-X.

This ready-reference tool evaluates and ranks more than 150 nations in 300 categories. Charts and graphs are provided. An excellent, initial reference for students.

Social Issues Resources Series (SIRS).
Boca Raton, FL: Social Issues Resources Series. Dates vary.
Number of pages varies. Prices range from $40 to $70.

The *Social Issues Resources Series* (SIRS) is designed to provide timely information on critical problems. The program consists of 32 titles in looseleaf volumes. Each volume contains reprints of newspaper and journal articles in their entirety. There are annual supplements. The programs in the series that may be of interest to students studying international issues are Pollution, Population, Women, Defense, Ethnic Groups, Food, Human Rights, and Third World.

World Economic Data: A Compendium of Current Economic Information for All Countries of the World.
Cecelia A. Albert, ed. Santa Barbara, CA: ABC-CLIO, 1987.
248p. $28.50. ISBN 0-87436-485-X.

Economic data on all countries of the world are provided in this factbook, which can be used by high school students. Included are data on budgets, GNP, imports/exports, tourism, energy, trade, labor, balance of payments, industrial and agricultural products, natural resources, and nuclear power. Also provided is a detailed section on U.S. economic indicators, a chart of world currency rates and conversions, a glossary, and a bibliography.

World Human Rights Guide.
Charles Humana. New York: Facts on File, 1985.
354p. $35. ISBN 0-8160-1404-3.

This handbook records and assesses the human rights performance of 120 countries relative to the Universal Declaration of Human Rights and United Nations treaties. Basic data are gathered from a 40-item questionnarie. Commentary and a basic data sheet for each country are provided.

World Tables: Volume 1, Economic Data.
Washington, DC: World Bank, 1984.
608p. $25. ISBN 0-8018-3201-2.

Data gathered and published by the World Bank are generally considered the most accurate economic data, especially on Third World and Communist countries. In Volume 1, three series of economic data sheets are provided on practically all countries of the world. The first series contains data on "Population, National Accounts, and Prices." The second series deals with balance of payments, external public debt, foreign trade indexes, and central government finances. Comparative economic data are provided in the third series.

Online Databases

The databases cited are available through one or more of the following services:

BRS Information Technologies
1200 Route 7
Latham, NY 12110
(800) 468-0908

CompuServe
5000 Arlington Center Boulevard
P.O. Box 20212
Columbus, OH 43220
(800) 848-8199

Dialog Information Services, Inc.
3460 Hillview Avenue
Palo Alto, CA 94304
(800) 3-DIALOG

Dow Jones News/Retrieval
P.O. Box 300
Princeton, NJ 08540
(609) 452-1511

ERIC
Supplier: Office of Educational Research and Information
Availability: BRS: $16–$35/hr.; citations: $.11 online, no offline charge

ERIC (Educational Resources Information Center) provides comprehensive coverage of all areas of education, including economics education. By searching this database, students and teachers can find journal articles, classroom materials, research reports, conference papers, and other materials dealing with economics, energy, population, environmental issues, foreign relations, peace education, and other economics-related fields and issues related to international studies.

Facts on File
Supplier: Facts on File, Inc.
Availability: DIALOG: $60/hr.; citations (full text): no online charge, $.25 offline

This database contains news summaries of worldwide economics, politics, government, business, medicine, sports, art, and more from worldwide news sources. By using the information, students will be able to track international news developments in economics.

Historical Abstracts
Supplier: ABC-CLIO
Availability: DIALOG: $65/hr.; citations: no online charge, $.15 offline

Articles appearing in almost 2,000 journals published worldwide on history since 1450, as well as related social sciences and humanities, are summarized and indexed. Also cites and indexes books and dissertations. Coverage includes economic and business history, political economy, and international economics and economic relations of the world outside the United States and Canada.

Japan Economic Daily
Supplier: Kyodo New International, Inc.
Availability: Dow Jones News/Retrieval: $.25/minute, academic rate

General Japanese economic, business, and political news as well as a review of the current day's top stories in Japan and reports on the Tokyo stock, bond, commodity, and currency markets. Students can use this database to research and analyze current events and international affairs in which Japan is an actor.

Magazine ASAP
Supplier: Information Access Company
Availability: BRS: $79-$98/hr.; citations (full text): $7 online, $7 offline
                 DIALOG: $84/hr.; citations (full text): $7 online, $7 offline

This database provides instant availability of magazine articles, editorials, columns, reviews, and product evaluations on a full range of topics, including international relations. It provides the full text and bibliographic information for articles published in more than 80 general-interest magazines. Coverage includes politics, economic relations, cultural exchange, and so on.

Magazine Index

Supplier: Information Access Company
Availability: BRS: $79–$98/hr.; citations: $.20 online, $.25 offline

DIALOG: $84/hr.; citations: $.10 online, $.20 offline

Articles, reviews, and features from more than 400 popular, general-interest U.S. magazines are indexed. Students will be able to use this file to locate articles dealing with international trade, negotiation, treaties, cultural exchange, world problems, and other global issues in magazines such as *Newsweek* or *Time.*

The Middle East: Abstracts and Index

Supplier: Northumberland Press
Availability: DIALOG: $55/hr.; citations: no online charge, $.25 offline

More than 1,500 English-language journals are indexed to provide coverage of 17 Middle East nations and the region. Subjects covered include business, current affairs, economics, education, government, religion, and politics. Students may refer to the database for current information and contemporary history of topics such as OPEC, the Iran-Iraq War, the Palestinian question, and so on.

National Newspaper Index

Supplier: Information Access Corporation
Availability: BRS: $79–$98/hr.; citations: $.20 online, $.25 offline

DIALOG: $84/hr.; citations: $.10 online, $.20 offline

Five major newspapers are indexed: the *Wall Street Journal,* the *New York Times,* the *Christian Science Monitor,* the *Los Angeles Times,* and the *Washington Post.* Every article and feature of each newspaper is covered. By using this database, students can keep up to date on current world events.

Newsearch

Supplier: Information Access Corporation
Availability: DIALOG: $120/hr.; citations: $.10 online, $.20 offline

This is the daily index to more than 2,000 news stories and other features from the following sources: newspapers from the *National Newspaper Index* (see preceding entry for description), popular magazines, trade and industry journals, complete press releases from PR Newswire, business and management journals, legal periodicals, and newspapers. The database will provide students with current news in the field of international issues and relations.

TASS
Supplier: Telegraph Agency of the Soviet Union (TASS)
Availability: CompuServe: $15/hr.; no offline prints

TASS contains the full text in English of all news reports from the official news agency of the Soviet Union. The news service covers political, economic, and cultural developments in the Soviet Union, international news, and analyses and commentaries of world events from the Soviet perspective.

Washington Post Electronic Edition
Supplier: Washington Post
Availability: DIALOG: $87/hr.; citations: $.25 online, $.25 offline

Dow Jones News/Retrieval: $.25/minute, academic rate

Complete texts of the daily and Sunday editions of the *Washington Post* newspaper are provided. Students may use the database to obtain quality coverage of international events.

World Affairs Report
Supplier: California Institute of International Studies
Availability: DIALOG: $90/hr.; citations: $.10 online, $.25 offline

This database covers worldwide news as perceived and reported by the Soviet Union. The Soviet point of view is contrasted with perspectives presented in a variety of Western publications, providing students with a unique opportunity to compare and analyze Western and Soviet reporting on specific issues.

Periodicals

ACCESS
The American Forum: Education in a Global Age and
The Council for Intercultural Studies and Programs
45 John Street, Suite 1200
New York, NY 10038
8 issues per year. $25/yr.

ACCESS provides current information on materials, events, and news related to global/international education and foreign languages. Social studies and foreign language teachers concerned with global perspectives will find this periodical essential.

Breakthrough
Global Education Associates
475 Riverside Drive, Suite 456
New York, NY 10115
Quarterly. $15 minimum contribution.

In addition to providing news of the association, resource lists, and reviews, each issue of *Breakthrough* focuses on a global theme, such as women around the world. Articles address the topic from different national and cultural perspectives.

Global Awareness
Global Awareness Program
College of Education
Florida International University
Tamiami Trail
Miami, FL 33199
Biannual. Free.

This newsletter describes programs, activities, credit courses, and resources for teaching global perspectives at the elementary and secondary levels. A special pull-out section in each issue contains classroom lesson plans.

Global Educator
Robert G. Hanvey
3463 State Street
Santa Barbara, CA 93105
8 issues per school year. $8/yr.

A short (4-page) monthly newsletter, *Global Educator* provides substantive coverage of issues in and resources for teaching global perspectives.

Global Pages
Immaculate Heart College Center
10951 W. Pico Boulevard, Suite 2021
Los Angeles, CA 90064
4 issues per year. $5/yr.

Each issue of *Global Pages* focuses on a specific theme relevant to classroom educators. Theoretical and practical articles are accompanied by resource lists and a calendar of events.

Interchange
Population Reference Bureau, Inc.
1337 Connecticut Avenue NW
Washington, DC 20036
Quarterly. One-year subscription free to educators.

Designed especially for teachers, this newsletter is accompanied twice a year by teaching modules on themes related to population issues.

Social Education
The National Council for the Social Studies
3501 Newark Street NW
Washington, DC 20016
7 times/yr. (September/October, November/December, January, February, March, April, and May). Members: $33/yr.; Nonmembers: $35/yr.

Social Education is the official journal of the National Council for the Social Studies. It contains both content articles and articles dealing with how and what to teach in the classroom. All of the social sciences, including economics, are treated. This journal is must reading for all economics teachers.

Update
Joint publication of the African, Asian, Latin American, and Russian/East European Center
University of Illinois
1208 W. California Street
Urbana, IL 61801
Quarterly. Free.

Each issue of the newsletter focuses on a specific theme, which is then treated from the context or perspective of each of the world culture areas. Past issues have focused on student life, constitutions, and minorities. Additionally, national and regional events and new resources are described.

World Eagle
World Eagle, Inc.
64 Washburn Avenue
Wellesley, MA 02181
Monthly throughout school year. $29.95/yr.

Each issue focuses on a global topic (e.g., human rights, food) and provides statistical data on that topic through charts, graphs, and maps, which are reproducible for classroom use. Highly useful both in terms of background information and classroom application.

Printed Indexes

Biography Index.
Bronx, NY: H.W. Wilson, 1946–   .
Quarterly. $75/yr.

This index is a guide to biographical materials appearing in periodicals and
books. It serves both general and scholarly reference needs. Students can
consult the index for the name of a particular national leader or international
actor.

Education Index.
Bronx, NY: H.W. Wilson, 1929–   .
*Monthly (September–June). Annual subscription rate determined by subscriber's
periodical holdings; minimum rate is $80.*

This is an author/subject index to periodicals in English that cover all levels
of education. Teachers in particular can use this index to locate reviews of
books, classroom materials, and ideas for classroom teaching.

Facts on File.
New York: Facts on File, 1940–   .
Weekly. $465/yr.

This index contains news summaries of worldwide economics, politics,
government, sports, art, and more from news sources around the world.
By using the information, students will be able to track international news
developments in economics.

Historical Abstracts.
Santa Barbara, CA: ABC-CLIO, 1955–   .
Historical Abstracts *is published in two parts*—Part A: Modern History
Abstracts, 1450 to 1914; Part B: Twentieth Century Abstracts, 1914 to
Present.
*The cost of all back volumes and of current volumes is based on the service rate
principle.*

Articles appearing in almost 2,000 journals published worldwide on history,
the social sciences, and related humanities are summarized and indexed by
subject and author. Since 1980, books and dissertations have also been cited
and indexed. Students and teachers will find this index useful for historical
research for all nations except the United States and Canada.

Reader's Guide to Periodical Literature.
Bronx, NY: H.W. Wilson, 1900–   .
Published 5 times/yr. (January, February, May, July, and August). $95.

Articles from popular, general interest U.S. magazines are subject indexed. Students can use this index to locate articles dealing with international relations, world environment, world problems, and other global issues in magazines such as *Newsweek* or *Time.*

Resources in Education.
Washington, DC: Superintendent of Documents, U.S. Government Printing Office, 1968.
Monthly. $56/yr.

This monthly index describes and subject indexes educational documents in all areas of education including economics, for all levels of education. For example, social studies teachers can use the index to locate international education research, papers delivered at conferences, classroom materials, and bibliographies of background readings. An advantage of this resource is that most items indexed are available in microfiche format in libraries in all parts of the country. In addition, most of the resources can be purchased in either microfiche or papercopy format.

Teacher Resource Materials

Anderson, Lee. **Schooling and Citizenship for a Global Age: An Exploration of the Meaning and Significance of Global Education.**
Bloomington, IN: Social Studies Development Center, 1979.
486p. $1.17 (microfiche) and $30 (paper copy) from the ERIC Document Reproduction Service.

This early work on global education documents the increasing globalization of society and describes changes within education that had already taken place in response to this trend in the late 1970s.

Bacckman, Earl R., ed. **Approaches to International Education.**
New York: Macmillan Publishing Co., 1984.
332p. $19.95. ISBN 0-02-901-360-7.

A total of 17 case studies clarifies how institutes of higher education have institutionalized their commitment to international education. Included in the study are eight state universities, six private colleges, and three community colleges.

Becker, James M. **Schooling for a Global Age.**
New York: McGraw-Hill, Inc., 1979.
345p. $16.95. ISBN 004-1903.

One of the first volumes to establish a rationale for global education and begin to define its content, this book provides an in-depth statement of the critical need for global education in U.S. elementary and secondary schools. Included in the volume are reviews of K–12 global education programs, strategies for curriculum planning and development, and resources available for program development. An extensive bibliography is included.

Dembo, David, ed. **Global Education at the Grass Roots: Profiles of School Based Programs.**
New York: Global Perspectives in Education, Inc. and the Council on International and Public Affairs, 1984.
170p. $20. ISBN 0-936876-18-2.

A total of 37 elementary and secondary programs in international and global education are profiled as a guide to educators interested in initiating like programs in their own schools or districts. Section one contains entries on each program. For each entry, the following information is provided: source of the program, methods of instruction, curriculum ideas, sources of district and community support, and staff development program. Section two briefly cites additional programs, including information on school, program title, address, phone number, and contact person.

Freeman, Robert E., ed. **Promising Practices in Global Education: A Handbook with Case Studies.**
New York: National Council on Foreign Languages and International Studies, 1986.
170p. $12.50. ISBN 0-944675-05-0.

This publication provides a rationale and a process for developing and implementing an international perspectives curriculum. Exemplary programs are described. Guides to developing local or district task forces to assure that programs are developed and implemented are provided.

Geography and International Knowledge.
Washington, DC: Association of American Geographers, 1982.
24p. $2.50. ISBN 0-89291-162-X.

This report explores the critical role that geography education plays in enhancing and expanding students' abilities to participate in an increasingly global society. The international content of geography education is defined as is the place of geography in the international studies curricula. Practical examples of the use of geographic knowledge in professions such as business and government are provided.

Hanvey, Robert G. **An Attainable Global Perspective. Occasional Paper No. 1.**
New York: Global Perspectives in Education, Inc., 1976.
28p. $2.

This brief publication offers a conceptual framework for including global perspectives in education. It presents a rationale, offers clear, concise reasons for the importance of global education, and provides strategies for integrating global education into the elementary and secondary curriculum.

International Dimensions of Education.
Washington, DC: Council of Chief State School Officers, 1985.
Free.

The Council of Chief State School Officers, a national membership organization of state-level educational administrators, reports on the status of international education. This paper establishes four international dimensions of education, sets goals for each of these dimensions, and recommends actions that can be taken at the national, state, and local level by government, institutes of higher education, and educational organizations to further these.

King, David, James Becker, and Larry Condon. **Education for a World in Change. A Report. Intercom 96/97.**
New York: Global Perspectives in Education, Inc., 1980.
61p. $5.

This volume presents a progress report on global education efforts and programs in U.S. elementary and secondary schools up to 1980. Separate sections focus on educational initiatives at the local level, an analysis of textbooks and supplementary classroom resource materials, and questions and answers about the field of global education.

Kniep, Willard, guest ed. **"Global Education: The Road Ahead,"** *Social Education* 50 no. 6 (October 1986): 415–452.

A special focus issue of the journal of the National Council for the Social Studies, this publication contains five articles that define the discipline of global education in the K–12 curriculum, provide a status report and rationale, and cite exemplary resource materials. A highly useful reading for social studies educators new to the field of global education.

Kniep, Willard, ed. **Next Steps in Global Education: A Handbook for Curriculum Development.**
New York: Global Perspectives in Education, 1987.
220p. $30. ISBN 0-944-675-01-8.

Designed as a practical aid to educators committed to infusing a global perspective throughout the curriculum, this loose-leaf volume provides a step-by-step guide to the process of developing sound and effective programs in global education. The handbook is a valuable resource for teachers, administrators, committees, task forces, and curriculum committees, whether they be interested in developing a single course or a comprehensive K–12 scope and sequence.

Lamy, Steven L., guest ed. **"Global Perspectives in Education,"** *Educational Research Quarterly* 8 no. 1 (1987).

This special theme issue contains 12 articles by experts in the field of global education. Articles focus on current content and pedagogical issues in global education, a review of the field, community connections, teaching, recent research, the impact of cross-cultural and travel experience on the teacher, global education in the curriculum, and consortia of global perspectives organizations.

Remy, Richard C., James A. Nathan, James M. Becker, and Judith V. Torney. **International Learning and International Education in a Global Age. Bulletin 47.**
Washington, DC: National Council for the Social Studies, 1975.
104p. $6.95.

This volume considers alternative world views and methods of teaching and learning about the world. Strategies and designs for world studies courses are provided, as is a bibliography and a set of guidelines for implementing international studies in the classroom.

Rosengren, Frank, Marylee Crofts Wiley, and David S. Wiley. **Internationalizing Your School: A Resource Guide for Teachers, Administrators, Parents, and School Board Members.**
New York: National Council on Foreign Language and International Studies, 1983.
63p. $7.50. ISBN 0-944675-04-2.

Designed to encourage the inclusion of international studies and foreign language programs in elementary and secondary schools, this publication recommends advocacy strategies for parents, school board members, school administrators, and teachers. Recommended background resources including books, articles, cassettes, and audiovisual materials are outlined, as are exemplary existing programs and curricula, K–12, from around the country.

Simon, Paul. **The Tongue-tied American: Confronting the Foreign Language Crisis.**
New York: Continuum Publishing Company, 1980.
224p. $12.95. ISBN 0-8264-0022-1.

Presents and analyzes the findings of several reports and studies of the President's Commission on Foreign Language and International Studies. Argues for the inclusion and enhancement of foreign language training programs within U.S. elementary and secondary schools in light of U.S. role in international affairs: government, economics, immigration, and so on.

The United States Prepares for Its Future: Global Perspectives in Education.
New York: Global Perspectives in Education, Inc., 1987.
52p. $10. ISBN 0-944675-08-5.

This volume presents the findings and recommendations of the Study Commission on Global Education. In addition to presenting a rationale for addressing global education in the K–12 curriculum, the Study Commission proposes changes in the existing curriculum that would increase the attention given to non-Western civilizations, world systems, and diverse cultural patterns both within and outside of the United States.

Classroom Materials

Computer Software

Annam: The Study of a Developing Country
Subject: Peace and security, development
Source: American Micro Media (distributor)
P.O. Box 306
Red Hook, NY 12571
(Producer: Educational Activities)
Cost: $63
Type: Simulation
Grades: 7–12
Systems: Apple II; Commodore 64; TRS 80

Students lead a developing nation, aided by a superpower, while pressured by an aggressive Communist neighbor. With numerous special interest groups and rivals galore, the leader must remain popular to govern. Decisions invariably lead to changes in the country's condition.

Balance of Power
Subject: Peace and security, development
Source: American Micro Media (distributor)
P.O. Box 306
Red Hook, NY 12571
(Producer: Mindscape)
Cost: $49.95
Type: Simulation game
Grades: 9–12
Systems: Apple II; IBM PC; Macintosh

Students play the role of either the president of the United States or the general secretary of the Soviet Union. While monitoring and responding to situations throughout the world, the goal is to enhance the home nation's prestige, without provoking nuclear war.

Beyond the Rising Sun: Discovering Japan
Subject: Development
Source: Social Studies School Service (distributor)
            10200 Jefferson Blvd.
            P.O. Box 802
            Culver City, CA 90232-0802
            (Producer: Educational Activities)
Cost: $63
Type: Tutorial game
Grades: 7–12
Systems: Apple II

Students play the role of a Japanese youth as they make decisions about the customs and habits of their character. Scored on three scales, success, money, and family harmony, student scores depend on how well they come to understand the Japanese culture.

BIFs: Basics in Forecasting (Population and Economic Models)
Subject: Development, peace and security
Source: Conduit
            University of Iowa, Oakdale Campus
            Iowa City, Iowa 52242
Cost: $75; $150, lab pack of 5 disks
Type: Simulation
Grades: 10–12
Systems: IBM PC with 192K

This package helps students make forecasts through a number of different models similar to ones in actual use by government and corporate officials.

COEXIST: Population Dynamics
Subject: Development
Source: Conduit
            University of Iowa, Oakdale Campus
            Iowa City, Iowa 52242
Cost: $45 (includes instructor's notes and students' leaflets);
            $90, lab pack of 5 disks
Type: Simulation
Grades: 10–12
Systems: Apple II

This unit simulates two biological situations. First, students model one or two populations to grow independently on separate but identical limited food resources. In the second model, students control parameters for competing populations.

Computer Diplomacy

Subject: Peace and security
Source: Social Studies School Service (distributor)
             10200 Jefferson Blvd.
             P.O. Box 802
             Culver City, CA 90232-0802
Cost: $50; $18, board game version
Type: Game
Grades: 9–12
Systems: IBM PC with 256K and color graphics card

This is a computerized version of the popular board game that realistically simulates diplomatic and military maneuvering of the Great Powers of Europe prior to and during World War I. Two or more players or teams may compete; three or more hours to complete.

Concepts Computerized Atlas

Subject: Development, environment
Source: Social Studies School Service (distributor)
             10200 Jefferson Blvd.
             P.O. Box 802
             Culver City, CA 90232-0802
             (Producer: Software Concepts)
Cost: $49.95; $2.95, teacher's guide
Type: Map database
Grades: 7–12
Systems: Apple II; IBM PC

This computerized atlas is a visual database, combining a three-dimensional globe with the information resources of an atlas. Includes data on every nation, all 50 states and more than 2,500 cities.

Decisions Decisions: Foreign Policy: The Burdens of World Power

Subject: Political systems, peace and security
Source: Tom Snyder Productions
             90 Sherman Street
             Cambridge, MA 02140
Cost: $89.95
Type: Simulation
Grades: 8–12
Systems: Apple II with 64K
             IBM PC with 128K, color graphics card

Students simulate leading a superpower while dealing with problems of foreign policy. A small but strategic nation requests aid in suppressing a popular rebellion. Should a nation get involved in the internal affairs of another nation? Only one computer is required to engage the entire class in this simulation.

Demo-Graphics
Subject: Development, environment
Source: Conduit
            University of Iowa, Oakdale Campus
            Iowa City, Iowa 52242
Cost: $85; $170, lab pack of 5 disks
Type: Simulation
Grades: 10–12
Systems: Apple II

The impact of real and simulated factors is modeled in this package on demographic dynamics. Data from 1980 on population, fertility, mortality, and cereal production are included for 40 nations.

Diffusion Game
Subject: Development, human rights
Source: Conduit
            University of Iowa, Oakdale Campus
            Iowa City, Iowa 52242
Cost: $55, $110, lab pack of 5 disks
Type: Simulation
Grades: 10–12
Systems: Apple II

Students learn about the diffusion of innovation among cultures as they assume the role of change agents attempting to convince rural villagers to adopt an innovation. Students must obtain information about the village culture and select effective diffusion methods to achieve success.

Ecological Modeling
Subject: Development, environment
Source: Conduit
            University of Iowa, Oakdale Campus
            Iowa City, Iowa 52242
Cost: $75; $150, lab pack of 5 disks
Type: Simulation
Grades: 10–12
Systems: Apple II; IBM PC

Students learn a variety of modeling techniques by controlling parameters in these seven programs simulating population growth in varying scenarios.

Endangered Species Databases
Subject: Environment
Source: Sunburst Communications (distributor)
             39 Washington Avenue, Room HG05
             Pleasantville, NY 10570-2898
Cost: $59; $177, lab pack of 10 disks
Type: Data files for database
Grades: 7–12
Systems: Apple II

These database files contain data on endangered species around the world, including those already extinct. The Bank Street School Filer is required to use these datafiles. The database disk can be copied.

Foreign Governments and United Nations
Subject: Peace and security
Source: Social Studies School Service (distributor)
             10200 Jefferson Blvd.
             P.O. Box 802
             Culver City, CA 90232-0802
             (Producer: SEI)
Cost: $39.95
Type: Drill and practice
Grades: 10–12
Systems: Apple II; IBM PC

This drill-and-practice program tests students on their knowledge of issues related to world affairs. Five tests cover the UN and UN organizations, seven tests cover various nations, and other tests examine monarchy, fascism, and socialism. Teachers may modify or delete existing tests or add new tests.

Global Mysteries: Map Skills
Subject: Development, environment
Source: Social Studies School Service (distributor)
             10200 Jefferson Blvd.
             P.O. Box 802
             Culver City, CA 90232-0802
             (Producer: Cram)
Cost: $39 (includes teacher's guide and reproducible student material)
Type: Tutorial game
Grades: 7–9
Systems: Apple II

Students pose as global detectives to solve mysteries by interpreting maps, tables, and graphs. Topics include latitude, longitude, directions, map scale, legends, and symbols.

IFs: International Futures Simulation

Subject: Peace and security, development, environment
Source: Conduit
University of Iowa, Oakdale Campus
Iowa City, Iowa 52242
Cost: $95; $190, lab pack of 5 disks
Type: Simulation
Grades: 10-12
Systems: IBM PC with 192K

Key issues of global development, its data and trends, and the connections among issues and regions are explored in this package. More than 50 variables can be controlled in making projections of the future.

Malthus

Subject: Development, environment
Source: Social Studies School Service (distributor)
10200 Jefferson Blvd.
P.O. Box 802
Culver City, CA 90232-0802
(Producer: Albion)
Cost: $39.95 (includes teacher's guide and reproducible handouts)
Type: Simulation
Grades: 10-12
Systems: Apple II

Based on the Club of Rome's computer model, and following a simple Malthusian framework, this program allows students to study the dynamics of exponential population growth and limited food resources.

Modern Eurasia

Subject: Peace and security, development, environment
Source: Focus Media, Inc.
839 Stewart Ave.
P.O. Box 865
Garden City, NY 11530
Cost: $99 (includes teacher's lesson planner and backup disks)
Type: Tutorial
Grades: 4-8
Systems: Apple II

Three programs teach the natural settings, history, and politics of modern Europe, modern Russia and Asia, and the modern Middle East.

Nationalism: Past and Present

Subject: Peace and security, development
Source: Focus Media, Inc.
          839 Stewart Ave.
          P.O. Box 865
          Garden City, NY 11530
Cost: $169
Type: Tutorial
Grades: 9–12
Systems: Apple II

This series of five programs helps students explore the roots of European nationalism, the process of nation-building, and destructive nationalism. Programs include "Nationalism: Its European Roots"; "Nation-Building: Graphing the Nation-Building Process"; "Destructive Nationalism"; and "Nationalism Today: The Soviet Union." An Instant Computerized Glossary is included to help students understand terms.

One World: Countries DataBase

Subject: Peace and security, development, environment
Source: Active Learning Systems
          P.O. Box 1984
          Midland, MI 48640
Cost: $148 (includes teacher's guide)
Type: Database
Grades: 7–12
Systems: Apple II

This program provides information on 178 nations in 33 categories of geography, economics, politics, and demographics. Teacher's guide includes reproducible activities, maps, and directions.

The Other Side: A Global Conflict Resolution Game

Subject: Peace and security
Source: Tom Snyder Productions
          90 Sherman Street
          Cambridge, MA 02140
Cost: $69.95, individual program; $210, lab pack of 10 disks and other
          materials
Type: Simulation
Grades: 5–12
Systems: Apple II with 64K; IBM PC with 128K and color graphics card

Two teams of students represent independent nations in a world of limited resources. They must develop appropriate strategies for maintaining a stable economy, military responsibility, and national security. This program can be used with one computer, with two connected computers, or with two computers connected via modem. A variety of cables for connecting computers is also available from Tom Snyder Productions.

Population Growth
Subject: Development, environment
Source: Conduit
University of Iowa, Oakdale Campus
Iowa City, Iowa 52242
Cost: $50; $100, lab pack of 5 disks
Type: Simulation
Grades: 10–12
Systems: Apple II

Intrinsic rate of natural increase, starting population, doubling time, and carrying capacity are all concepts introduced to students in this package. Students learn the geometric growth ratio to predict population size.

Revolutions: Past, Present, Future
Subject: Peace and security, development
Source: Focus Media, Inc.
839 Stewart Ave.
P.O. Box 865
Garden City, NY 11530
Cost: $169 (includes teacher's lesson planner)
Type: Tutorial
Grades: 9–12
Systems: Apple II; TRS-80

Students are introduced to the concept of revolution through a series of five programs. Titles include "What is a Revolution?"; "Historical Models of Revolutions"; "How to Analyze a Revolution"; "Graphing Revolutions of the Past"; and "Graphing Revolutions of the Present and Future." Teacher's lesson planner includes ideas, worksheets, and teaching suggestions.

Rice Farming
Subject: Development
Source: Social Studies School Service (distributor)
10200 Jefferson Blvd.
P.O. Box 802
Culver City, CA 90232-0802
(Producer: Longman Resource Unit)
Cost: $59.95
Type: Simulation
Grades: 7–12
Systems: Apple II

Students become rice farmers in India, facing problems and making decisions similar to those experienced in developing nations. Faced with such problems as droughts, pest infestations, and inflation, they must decide what variety of rice to plant, how much rice to grow and market, and whether to purchase a well, fertilizer, or pesticides.

R.S.V.P.
Subject: Peace and security, development
Source: American Micro Media (distributor)
             P.O. Box 306
             Red Hook, NY 12571
             (Producer: Blue Lion Software Corporation)
Cost: $39.95, Apple II/IBM
             $29.95, Commodore 64
Type: Tutorial/simulation
Grades: 7-12
Systems: Apple II; IBM PC with color graphics card; Commodore 64

In this program students encounter more than 700 tricky cultural situations as they learn about national and international manners and customs from 17 categories and 18 nations.

Satellite Down: Rescue Adventures in Geography—World Edition
Subject: Environment, development
Source: Social Studies School Service (distributor)
             10200 Jefferson Blvd.
             P.O. Box 802
             Culver City, CA 90232-0802
             (Producer: Focus Media)
Cost: $85 (includes lesson planner)
Type: Tutorial game
Grades: 7-9
Systems: Apple II

Students test their knowledge of the world by trying to locate a downed satellite, based on clues concerning the region in which it crashed. Clues include radio and TV broadcasts, local climate conditions, flora and fauna, economic activity, transportation systems, and native landmarks. Difficulty level can be adjusted. Includes a wall map and student maps.

Scholastic pfs: World Geography
Subject: Development, environment
Source: Scholastic Inc.
             P.O. Box 7502
             2931 East McCarty Street
             Jefferson City, MO 65102

Cost: $79.95
Type: Data files for database
Grades: 7-12
Systems: Apple II with 64K; IBM PC with 128K

This set of data disks for use with the Scholastic pfs:File and pfs:Report programs contains hundreds of facts about land, people, work, and transportation around the world.

Simpolecon
Subject: Development
Source: Cross Cultural Software
            5385 Elrose Avenue
            San Jose, CA 95124
Cost: $120
Type: Simulation
Grades: 10-12
Systems: Apple II and IIe with two disk drives

This simulation is a complex, realistic portrayal of the processes and problems of national economic development. It teaches about the international aspects of growth and stability. Students are their country's decision makers. At the start each country receives a limited amount of productive resources. Students must create and maintain a stable, secure country with a well-balanced economy.

Social Studies Tool Kit: The World: An Introduction to Social Data Processing
Subject: Peace and security, development, environment, human rights
Source: Great Lakes Software
            P.O. Box 8756
            Green Bay, WI 54308
Cost: $89
Type: Database
Grades: 7-12
Systems: Apple II

This database program is especially noteworthy for its excellent sections on the meaning and interpretation of the data. Samples are discussed and materials are provided for teaching about the analysis of social data. Data are included for 151 nations. Data can be searched and reported numerous ways.

Survival: Simulation of Survival of the Fittest
Subject: Peace and security, development, environment, human rights

Source: American Micro Media (distributor)
             P.O. Box 306
             Red Hook, NY 12571
             (Producer: Krell)
Cost: $49.95
Type: Simulation
Grades: 7–12
Systems: Apple II

Survival of the fittest and Social Darwinism are central concepts addressed in this program. Survival is difficult as changes occur in the environment. Parameters and patterns can be altered for experimentation.

Travels with Za-Zoom: The World
Subject: Development, environment
Source: Social Studies School Service (distributor)
             10200 Jefferson Blvd.
             P.O. Box 802
             Culver City, CA 90232-0802
             (Producer: Focus Media)
Cost: $85 (includes teacher's guide and handouts)
Type: Tutorial game
Grades: 4–8
Systems: Apple II; IBM PC

Students visit mystery locations and determine where they are by selecting clues on two levels. Clues include landmarks, bodies of water, weather, clothing, food, or other cultural activity. Includes a map and suggested activities.

The United Nations Classroom
Subject: Peace and security, development, environment, human rights
Source: Global Education Motivators, Inc.
             Montgomery County Intermediate Building
             Montgomery Avenue & Paper Mill Road
             Erdenheim, PA 19118
Cost: $800/yr.
Type: Computerized bulletin board
Grades: 7–12
Systems: All

This is a computer bulletin board program that gives users information on a major global issue each month. Each topic is presented in 8 to 10 pages with student activities and resources. A set of 25 databases is sold on a yearly subscription basis. Hard copies may be obtained.

War or Peace? You Decide!: Decision-Making in Nuclear Age
Subject: Peace and security
Source: Social Studies School Service (distributor)
             10200 Jefferson Blvd.
             P.O. Box 802
             Culver City, CA 90232-0802
             (Producer: Bright Ideas)
Cost: $59.95 (includes teacher's manual, lesson plans, and reproducible
             student guide)
Type: Simulation
Grades: 7-12
Systems: Apple II; IBM PC

By assuming the perspective of either superpower, students attempt to react
to quickly changing events in various potential world flashpoints.

Where in the World Is Carmen Sandiego?
Subject: Peace and security, environment
Source: Broderbund
             17 Paul Drive
             San Rafael, CA 94903-2101
Cost: $49.95, Apple II/Macintosh/IBM; $99.95, lab pack of 5 disks
             $44.95, Commodore; $89.95, lab pack of 5 disks
             (includes teacher's guide)
Type: Game
Grades: 4-9
Systems: Apple II; Macintosh; IBM PC; Commodore 64/128

Tracking down and arresting international criminals teaches students
facts about 30 great cities and nations of the world. Students also learn
rudimentary database operation, as well as geography, history, economics,
and cultural information.

Who'll Save Abacaxi?: A Third World Government Simulation
Subject: Peace and security, development, human rights
Source: Focus Media, Inc.
             839 Stewart Avenue
             P.O. Box 865
             Garden City, NY 11530
Cost: $65 (includes teacher's lesson planner and student workbook)
Type: Simulation
Grades: 7-12
Systems: Apple II

Students simulate running the government of a new, troubled country, while
analyzing various development strategies and making difficult decisions.

World Geography Explorer Series

Subject: Development, environment
Source: Social Studies School Service (distributor)
             10200 Jefferson Blvd.
             P.O. Box 802
             Culver City, CA 90232-0802
             (Producer: Mindscape)
Cost: $39.95 each; $150 complete series of four units (includes
             teacher's guide and reproducible activity sheets)
Type: Tutorial game
Grades: 5–8
Systems: Apple II

Students use deductive reasoning skills to determine where they are, obtaining clues from on-screen objects or interviews with characters they meet, as they explore each of these disks. Advanced and beginning levels can be selected, and the program will track 50 students.

World Geography Trivia

Subject: Environment
Source: Social Studies School Service (distributor)
             10200 Jefferson Blvd.
             P.O. Box 802
             Culver City, CA 90232-0802
             (Producer: Educational Activities)
Cost: $40
Type: Tutorial game
Grades: 7–12
Systems: Apple II

High resolution graphics and a clue system help students answer questions about the six inhabited continents.

Multimedia Kits

Close Up Special Focus: U.S./Soviet Relations.
Washington, DC: Close Up Foundation, 1986.
Kit containing a videocassette, student paperback, and teacher's guide: $199.
Subject: Global political systems; global peace and security issues.

Student readings support four 30-minute video programs on the complex relationship between the world's two superpowers. Each program focuses on a specific topic and includes a short documentary background and a question-answer session between high school students and experts. Footage is taken from photographs, films, and Close Up student seminars. Topics explored are the history of U.S.-Soviet relations, foreign policy administration, the arms race, and the future relations between the superpowers.

Comparative World Religions.
New York: Educational Enrichment, no date.
Kit containing 6 color filmstrips, 6 cassettes, and guide: $150.
Subject: Human values.

Provides an overview of each of the world's major religions, including the basic beliefs and practices, origins, and founders. Religions addressed are Hinduism, Judaism, Buddhism, Confucianism, Taoism, Shintoism, Christianity, and Islam. Commonalities and differences among the religions are also examined. A teacher's guide includes basic activities and discussion questions.

Exploring Political Terrorism.
Pleasantville, NY: Human Relations Media, 1983.
Kit containing 3 filmstrips, 3 cassettes, and teacher's guide: $155. Also available in videocassette: $165.
Subject: Global peace and security issues; human rights.

Provides complete materials for an intensive unit on political terrorism. Part 1 examines tactics, methods, and organization. Part 2 provides a historical overview of terrorism and offers profiles of terrorist groups around the world, including the Palestine Liberation Organization, labor unions, the Irish Republican Army, neo-Nazis, and the Red Brigade. Part 3 uses a fictional hostage simulation to help students explore techniques used by governments and private organizations to combat terrorism.

Food First.
Oley, PA: Bullfrog Films, 1980.
Kit containing a filmstrip and 2 cassettes: $75. Also available as 270 color slides: $135.
Subject: Global economic systems; development issues.

In Part I, "Why Hunger," students learn that the real cause of hunger is the increasing concentration of control over food-producing resources. Part II, "Towards Food Security," discusses the inefficiency and inequality of the present system and shows how people all over the world are working to gain control over their own food resources.

The Global Community.
Niles, IL: United Learning, 1985.

Kit containing 4 color filmstrips and 4 cassettes, with guide: $145. Also available in VHS format.
Subject: Global economic, ecological, and technological systems.

This multimedia program introduces students to the concept of interdependence and provides an analysis of the positive and negative effects of such interdependence. Specific topics covered include resource allocation, technology, agriculture, and communication. Lesson plans, discussion questions, and extension activities are provided in the accompanying guide.

How to Study Cultures.
Niles, IL: United Learning Corp., no date.
Kit containing 8 filmstrips, 8 cassettes, 1 teacher's guide, and a set of duplicating masters: $240.
Subject: Human values.

Recommended for junior high school through college, this program focuses on basic aspects of human culture as seen by cultural anthropologists. Examples of universal human behavior are drawn from a variety of cultures on six continents. Major topics covered are the concept of culture, the anthropological study of culture, the effect of environment on culture, how cultures meet economic needs, cultural beliefs and value systems, forms of communication, social organization, and the process of change within and across cultures.

International Relations: Understanding the Behavior of Nations.
Washington, DC: Close Up Foundation, 1988.
Kit including a 60-minute color VHS cassette, 25 student paperbacks, and 2 teacher's guides: $199.
Subject: Global political systems; global peace and security issues.

A coordinated video and print unit helps students understand the process of international policymaking. Students read and view interviews with politicians and diplomats as they explore topics such as the pursuit of national self-interest, East-West tensions, the making of U.S. foreign policy, and interdependence of nations.

Population Growth Rate Poster Kit.
Washington, DC: The World Bank, 1987.
Kit containing colored poster map of the world, 6 color photographs, and a teaching guide: $6.50.
Subject: Global economic systems; development issues.

Topics covered through this poster kit program are Third World family planning, why people in poorer countries tend to have larger families, and how to read statistics.

Relations of Nations: 20th Century Intervention.
New York: Random House Media, 1986.
Kit containing 6 color filmstrips, 6 cassettes, and accompanying guide: $165.
Subject: Global economic and political systems; global peace and security
issues.

This series helps secondary school students understand both the motivations
and methods of powerful nations that intervene in the internal affairs of
other nations. Through a historical survey, the program documents three
reasons for intervention—security, profit, and ideology—and three means of
intervention—military force, economic domination, and propaganda. The
program provides case studies representing each world region, including the
United States, the Soviet Union, European nations, Asian powers, and
developing nations.

Toward a Better World.
Washington, DC: The World Bank, 1980–1986.

Components are:

> *The Developing World.* Includes student book, *The Developing World,*
> 104p; two sound filmstrips, *Some Big Questions* and *Toward a Better*
> *World;* and a teaching guide, 116p with 30 worksheets: $75.

> *The Rajasthan Canal Project.* Includes a student pamphlet, *Economic*
> *Summary: India,* 8p; a student book, *The Rajasthan Canal Project,* 40p;
> a sound filmstrip, *What Happens When a Desert Blooms;* and a teaching
> guide, 52p with 12 worksheets: $60.

> *Small-Scale Industries in Kenya.* Includes a student pamphlet, *Economic*
> *Summary: Kenya,* 8p; a student book, *Small-Scale Industries in Kenya,*
> 48p, and a sound filmstrip of the same title; and a teaching guide, 52p
> with 12 worksheets: $60.

> *Tackling Poverty in Rural Mexico.* Includes a student pamphlet,
> *Economic Summary: Mexico,* 8p; a student book, *Tackling Poverty*
> *in Rural Mexico,* 48p; sound filmstrip, *Many Steps, One Goal;* and
> a teaching guide, 52p with 12 worksheets: $60.

> *Improving Indonesia's Cities.* Includes a student pamphlet, *Economic*
> *Summary: Indonesia,* 8p; a student book, *Improving Indonesia's Cities,*
> 56p; a sound filmstrip, *Building and Rebuilding;* and a teaching guide,
> 100p with 25 worksheets: $60.

All six filmstrips from the kits are also available for individual purchase. Each
filmstrip comes with an audiocassette, complete script, and teaching activity.
Set of six filmstrips: $100. Individual filmstrips: $20.

Toward a Better World is a multimedia kit for secondary school students that
deals with world poverty and economic and social changes that must be
made to relieve it. Students learn the differences between developing and

developed countries and then study the economies of India, Kenya, Mexico, and Indonesia.

Toxic Wastes.
Madison, WI: Hawkhill, 1984.
Kit containing 2 color filmstrips, 2 cassettes, and guide: $86. Also available on videocassette with guide: $118.
Subject: Global ecological systems; global environmental problems.

This two-part unit presents the history and the current state of the toxic waste problem in global perspective. The first program puts the problem in perspective by presenting background on toxic wastes from the Roman Empire, medieval Europe, and the Industrial Revolution. The program emphasizes progress by key figures such as Louis Pasteur and Edward Jenner. The second program educates students in basic scientific concepts surrounding toxic waste.

Who Owns the Oceans?
Ridgefield, CT: Current Affairs, no date.
Kit including 1 filmstrip, 1 cassette, and teacher's guide: $35.
Subject: Global ecological systems.

The world's oceans are an important source of food and mineral wealth. This program illustrates why and how nations with access to the oceans seek to maximize their claim to its resources, while also showing the concern of landlocked and less-developed nations over a share of the ocean's wealth. Discusses the issues and perspectives involved in international regulation of the oceans.

Why Cultures Are Different.
Niles, IL: United Learning, no date.
Kit containing 6 color filmstrips, 3 cassettes, and guide: $165.
Subject: Human values.

A comparative survey of cultural traits around the world is provided in this program. Students examine factors that contribute to cultural differences, including history, geography, language, and religion. Guide includes program script, study questions, and activity suggestions.

Women in World Area Studies.
Minneapolis: Glenhurst Publications, 1986.
Each kit in the series contains a filmstrip, cassette, reader, and teacher's guide: $38. Total: 7 kits.
Subject: Human rights; global history.

Each of the multimedia programs in this series provides comprehensive historical and contemporary coverage of the roles of women within a given country or culture area. Programs in the series look at women in China, the Middle East (Islam and Israel), India, the Soviet Union, Africa, Japan, and Latin America.

World Resources and Responsibilities.
Culver City, CA: Social Studies School Service, 1976.
Kit containing two color filmstrips and two cassettes: $79.
Subject: Global economic systems; development issues.

Students are asked to examine the world situation in which some nations are very wealthy with many resources whereas other nations do not have enough food to feed their growing population. Students discuss global economic interdependence and consider the practical and ethical positions of wealthy nations.

Simulations and Games

Bafa Bafa
Subject:	Human values
Grades:	8–12
Playing time:	2–3 class periods
Participants:	18–36
Cost:	$69.50
Publisher:	Simile II
	Box 910
	Del Mar, CA 92104

In *Bafa Bafa*, students adopt the characteristics and values of two hypothetical and contrasting cultures. They then visit the opposite culture to observe, interact with, and collect data on the characteristics of that culture. This is an excellent simulation for helping students understand the meaning of culture, the formation of stereotypes, and the difficulties of cross-cultural communication. An adapted version of this simulation, called *Rafa Rafa*, is suitable for younger students and is available for $25.

Creative Role-Playing Exercises in Science and Technology
Subject:	Global ecological systems; global environmental issues
Grades:	9–12
Playing time:	5–10 class periods
Participants:	20–35

Cost: $24.95
Publisher: Social Science Education Consortium, Inc.
               855 Broadway
               Boulder, CO 80302

This book contains all materials for five separate simulations that involve students as decision makers in public policy issues related to science and technology. Students must conduct research, analyze source material, develop position statements, work cooperatively in groups, and make and defend decisions. Simulations in the book with an international focus look at acid rain controversies between the United States and Canada and international access to ocean mineral resources.

Global Futures Game
Subject: Global economic systems
Grades: 9–college
Playing time: 3 class periods
Participants: 6–48 players
Cost: $17.75
Publisher: Social Studies School Service (distributor)
                 10200 Jefferson Boulevard
                 P.O. Box 802
                 Culver City, CA 90232-0802

In this simulation, students take the roles of decision makers from each of the world's regions. Over nine rounds, the teams trade, negotiate, and make plans for their futures. The goal for each team (world region) is to maintain or achieve an adequate lifestyle for its people by gaining or limiting population, selling or buying food, and advancing or limiting technological development. Suitable for global education, world culture, and world geography courses, as well as specific area studies courses.

Heelotia: A Cross-Cultural Simulation
Subject: Human values
Grades: 7–12
Playing time: Flexible
Participants: Two teams of flexible numbers
Cost: $2.95
Publisher: Stanford Program on International and Cross-Cultural
                 Education
                 Littlefield Center, Room 14
                 Stanford University
                 Stanford, CA 94305-5013

Students are divided into two hypothetical cultures to gain first-hand experience in the formulation of stereotypes, perceptions, and misperceptions. Over several rounds of play, each culture sends representatives to observe and try to interact with the opposite culture. This simulation is an excellent introduction to the study of other cultures or to orientation for travel/study experiences abroad.

International Trade

Subject:	Global economic systems
Grades:	10–12
Playing time:	2–5 hours
Participants:	Teams of 6
Cost:	$16.30
Publisher:	Didactic Systems, Inc.
	P.O. Box 457
	Crawford, NJ 07016

Students role play competitive importers, exporters, traders, and bankers, all trying to gain profits from trade. Although designed primarily for economics courses, the simulation may be helpful to students studying international economic relations in a variety of world-focused courses.

Judgement

Subject:	Human rights; global history
Grades:	10–12
Playing time:	10 class periods
Participants:	Up to 35
Cost:	$16
Publisher:	Interact
	P.O. Box 997F
	Lakeside, CA 92040

Students simulate a hypothetical trial of President Harry Truman following World War II. Truman is on trial as a war criminal for his decision to drop the world's first atomic bombs on Hiroshima and Nagasaki, Japan. Students take the roles of members of an international tribunal, President Truman, prosecution and defense counsels, and witnesses for both sides. Students must research the historical period, the international players, and then consider moral, ethical, and practical issues surrounding the decision to drop the bomb. Because students are asked to take the roles of Japanese and other nations directly and indirectly affected by the decision to drop the bomb, this is an excellent simulation for developing global perspectives in world history.

Living in a Global Age

Subject:	Global economic systems; global development issues
Grades:	7–12
Playing time:	2–3 class periods
Participants:	3 groups of 4–10 players each

Cost: $6.50
Publisher: Stanford Program on International and Cross-Cultural
               Education
               Littlefield Center, Room 14
               Stanford University
               Stanford, CA 94305-5013

Students divided into three groups must assemble working flashlights in this simulation of international trade and communication. Student groups simulate the cooperation and conflict that arise among energy-rich nations, technology-rich nations, and developed and developing countries of today. Suitable for world culture and geography courses, economics courses, and international relations courses.

Map Games (series)
Subject: Global economic systems; global technological systems;
                 global environmental issues
Grades: 7–12
Playing time: Flexible
Participants: 2–30
Cost: *World Economy Game:* $17
                 Energy-Producing Nations: $17
Source: Social Studies School Service (distributor)
                 10200 Jefferson Boulevard
                 P.O. Box 802
                 Culver City, CA 90232-0802
                 (Publisher: Charlottesville, VA: Educational Materials
                 Associates)

As they develop their skills in world geography, students learn about the world economy. The first game deals with the world economy, the second with global energy resources. Appropriate for economics, world cultures, and world geography courses.

Simulations for a Global Perspective
Subject: Global systems and issues; human values
Grades: 7–12
Playing time: Variable
Participants: Variable
Cost: $7
Publisher: Global Perspectives in Education, Inc.
                 45 John St., Suite 1200
                 New York, NY 10038

This print publication contains several complete simulation games compiled from a collection of issues of *Intercom.* Simulations focus on a variety of topics including the global environment. They are suitable for the entire range of secondary social studies offerings, including world cultures and world history classes, current events, and so on.

Skyjack

Subject:	Global peace and security issues
Grades:	7-12
Playing time:	8-10 class periods
Participants:	20-35
Cost:	$16
Publisher:	Interact
	P.O. Box 997F
	Lakeside, CA 92040

Students act as national leaders and cabinet ministers from five imaginary nations who must select a plan of action to ensure the safe release of their own citizens aboard a hijacked jet. Through successive rounds, the terrorists make new demands on the five countries and student players must respond. Students are called upon to analyze maps and statistical data, record notes, make group decisions, and synthesize information. Useful for helping students develop an appreciation of cross-cultural perspectives and conflicting national viewpoints and needs. Appropriate for world cultures, world geography, U.S. foreign policy, and current events courses.

The Stock Market Game

Subject:	Global economic systems
Grades:	5-8
Playing time:	8-10 hours
Participants:	15-25
Cost:	$18.50
Publisher:	Interact
	P.O. Box 997F
	Lakeside, CA 92040

Students first do research and class projects on stock prices, market fluctuation, stock transactions, and balancing bank accounts. The second phase—the simulation—involves students in playing the stock market.

Teaching About Global Awareness with Simulations and Games

Subject:	Global issues and systems; human values
Grades:	7-12
Playing time:	Varies
Participants:	Varies

Cost: $21.95
Publisher: Center for Teaching International Relations
                 University of Denver
                 Denver, CO 80208

This publication contains a set of simulations on a variety of topics including ethnic identity, food distribution, inequality, economic interdependence, and war. Appropriate for a wide range of social studies courses.

Where in the World?
Subject: Global economic systems, global political systems
Grades: 3–12
Playing time: Flexible
Participants: 2–6 players
Cost: $8 per game set, one set for each continent
Publisher: Aristoplay
                 P.O. Box 7028
                 Ann Arbor, MI 48107

This series of board games helps students develop geographical knowledge and global awareness. Each game package comes with six question sets, each for a different skill level. Students learn names of countries, locations, significant facts, and historical and contemporary events. Appropriate for world cultures, world geography, and area studies courses.

Wildfire II: A Learning Game on the Spread of Nuclear Weapons
Subject: Global political systems; global peace and security issues
Grades: 9–12
Playing time: 3 class periods
Participants: Up to 30 players
Cost: $29.95
Publisher: Social Studies School Service (distributor)
                 10200 Jefferson Boulevard
                 P.O. Box 802
                 Culver City, CA 90232-0802

Students play the leaders and their advisors of world superpower nations and their allies to handle an international crisis along the India-Pakistan border before it becomes a global nuclear war. Students are introduced to the issues surrounding nuclear proliferation and conflicting national interest. Players proceed through three rounds: introduction, crisis control, and negotiation. Appropriate for area studies and world cultures/geography courses, as well as international relations or nuclear education courses.

World: A Simulation of How Nations Develop and Become Involved in Power Struggles

Subject:	Global political systems; global peace and security issues
Grades:	7–10
Playing time:	25 class periods
Participants:	25–35
Cost:	$40
Publisher:	Interact
	P.O. Box 997F
	Lakeside, CA 92040

Although quite long, this simulation will be useful in helping students understand the stages of national development. Students create their own nation, select a form of government, and acquire power in the international arena through projects that accumulate points. Appropriate in world culture, geography, and history courses.

Supplementary Print Materials

Adelfang, Karen, et al. **Law Around the World.**
Boulder, CO: Safeguard Law Related Education Program, 1985.
570p. $24.95.
Subject: Human values, human rights issues, global history.

This supplement to law or world studies courses contains teacher material and student activities on the origins and development of law in seven countries that represent distinctive legal traditions: Venezuela, South Africa, the United Kingdom, Canada, the Soviet Union, Saudi Arabia, and China. A culminating section focuses on strategies for comparing law and legal traditions across cultures.

Anderson, Charlotte, guest ed. **Through the Legal Looking Glass: Reflections of Peoples and Cultures.** *Intercom 100.*
New York: Global Perspectives in Education, 1981.
40p. $8.
Subject: Human values, human rights issues.

This publication contains teacher background readings and student lessons for infusing a global perspective into the study of law. An introductory essay provides a rationale for a global approach to law. It is followed by lessons on the history of written law in Western civilization, literature as a vehicle for examining law in African cultures, and the cultural context of Chinese law. Bibliographies are included.

Backler, Alan, ed. **The Geographic Route to a Global Perspective.**
Intercom 101.
New York: Global Perspectives in Education, 1982.
40p. $4.
Subject: Global ecological systems.

A total of 11 classroom lessons are arranged sequentially to develop
an understanding of the effects of culture on human perception of and
relationship to the environment. Students explore the relationship between
survival needs and environment and cultural perceptions of basic needs.

Benegar, John. **Teaching Writing Skills. A Global Approach.**
Denver, CO: Center for Teaching International Relations, 1986 (rev.).
189p. $21.95. ISBN 0-943804-39-6.
Subject: Human values.

A total of 30 activities for grades 7–12 help students improve writing skills.
The activities take a unique approach by using global issues as a focus on
writing activities. Students simultaneously learn about interdependence,
perception, conflict, cultural awareness, language, and human rights.

Broken Squares.
Stanford, CA: Stanford Program on International and Cross-Cultural
Education, no date.
13p. $2.95.
Subject: Human values.

This brief activity helps secondary students explore the concept of
cooperation, relating the concept to social organizations in general and
to contemporary Chinese society in particular.

Cornish, Edward, ed. **Global Solutions. Innovative Approaches to World
Problems.**
Bethesda, MD: World Future Society, 1984.
160p. $6.95. ISBN 0-930242-22-X.
*Subject: Global economic, political, ecological, and technological systems; peace
and security issues; development issues.*

A selection of articles from *The Futurist* focuses on current world issues.
Topics covered are people power, housing for the future, backyard gardens,
expanding human intelligence, information technology, health care, food,
images of global governance, conflict and conflict resolution, macro-
engineering, space, multinational corporations, agriculture, solar power, and
sustainable society. This publication may be a useful supplement for high
school courses infusing a global perspective.

Croddy, Marshall, and Phyllis Maxey. **International Law in a Global Age.**
Los Angeles: Constitutional Rights Foundation, 1982.
Student book, 96p, and teacher's handbook, 159p. $17.50.
Subject: Human values; human rights issues; global political systems.

A supplementary program to infuse a global approach into law-related
education or law into global studies, *International Law in a Global Age*
contains five units of activities. An introductory unit helps students develop
an understanding of the global community—the connections among
different peoples and cultures and the problems they share. Succeeding units
focus on cultural contrasts, actors and relationships, the world order, and
conflict and its resolution in the world arena. This program may also serve
as the basal curriculum for a semester course on international law.

Demystifying the Chinese Language.
Stanford, CA: Stanford Program on International and Cross-Cultural
Education, 1984.
139p. $19.95.
Subject: Human values; global history.

By exploring the origins and development of the Chinese pictograph and
ideograph writing system, students gain an understanding and appreciation
of the cultural context and logic of a foreign language. Students apply what
they have learned through deciphering and writing activities.

The Development Data Book.
Washington, DC: The World Bank, 1984.
Student book, 16p, and teaching guide, 40p. $10. ISBN 0-8213-0312-0
(student) and 0-8213-0313-9 (teacher).
Subject: Global economic systems; development issues.

Designed to be used as either a reference tool or a teaching unit, this
program contains maps, charts, tables, and readings to help students develop
understanding of the concepts of life expectancy, literacy, population growth
rate, gross national product, and export trade in global perspective. Activities
are provided for different ability levels; tests are included.

Eddinger, Suzanne S. **Global Economics for Middle and Secondary Students.**
Athens, GA: University of Georgia Center for Economics Education, 1983.
131p. ED 245 987. Available in microfiche ($.75) or paper copy ($10.80) plus
postage from the ERIC Document Reproduction Service.
Subject: Global economic systems.

Sixteen detailed lessons introduce concepts of global economics. Major
topics covered are imports, unequal resources, scarcity, interdependence,
free trade versus protectionism, international finance, and monetary systems.

Elder, Pamela, and Mary A. Carr. **Worldways: Bringing the World into the Classroom.**
Menlo Park, CA: Addison-Wesley, 1987.
251p. $22.50. ISBN 0-201-22126-8.
Subject: Global economic, ecological, and technical systems; human values.

More than 75 activities and activity ideas are provided to help teachers infuse global education into a wide variety of disciplines. Activities are especially well suited for middle school grades. Activities focus on food, environment, shelter, travel, and so on. Appendices include a bibliography and a list of embassies and tourist offices.

Franz, Del. **Exploring the Third World: Development in Africa, Asia, and Latin America.**
New York: Global Perspectives in Education, 1987.
10 student handbooks, 44p, teacher's guide, 28p, and wall map. $35.
ISBN 0944675-18-2.
Subject: Global development issues.

This unit is designed to help secondary students understand development issues in the Third World. Students begin by examining connections between U.S. communities and the Third World, then go on to explore problems of less-developed nations. Issues covered include economic growth, the environment, population growth, alternative development strategies, and economic interdependence. The unit includes readings, activities, charts, graphs, maps, and simulations and is appropriate for programs in world history, area studies, world geography, and economics.

The Global Product: Internationalization of the Auto Industry.
Stanford, CA: Stanford Program on International and Cross-Cultural Education, 1987.
43p. $9.95.
Subject: Global economic systems; development issues.

Students role-play various interest groups as they examine both the process of car manufacturing and the decisions involved in international production of the product.

Global 2000 Countdown Kit.
Washington, DC: Zero Population Growth, 1982.
Box of 14 study activities. $20.
Subject: Global development issues; global economic and ecological systems.

Based on the *Global 2000 Report to the President,* this kit contains activities designed for independent student research and study. Each activity focuses on a single topic of the report, such as population, income, energy, resources, and environmental trends. Students collect and analyze data, conduct library research, and debate ideas.

Graves, Norman, O. J. Dunlop, and Judith Torney-Purta, eds. **Teaching for International Understanding, Peace, and Human Rights.**
New York: UNESCO, 1984.
244p. $18.75. ISBN 92-3-102098-6.
Subject: Human values; human rights.

More than 20 activities are designed to raise students' sensitivity to international human rights issues. Activities are presented in three categories: basic human rights concepts, organizations and institutions that deal with human rights issues, and problems caused by the denial of human rights. All student and teacher materials are included.

Gross, Susan, and Marjorie Bingham. **Toward Achieving Historical Symmetry: A Manual for Teaching Women's History.**
Santa Rosa, CA: National Women's History Project, 1983.
107p. $9.95.
Subject: Human values, human rights, development issues.

This teacher's manual presents three models for adopting a cross-cultural approach to women's studies. A framework for teaching women's history in a global setting, and lessons to introduce students to researching women's history are also provided.

Haas, John D., et al. **Teaching About the Future. Tools, Topics, and Issues for the Future.**
Boulder, CO: Social Science Education Consortium and Center for Teaching International Relations, 1987.
171p. $19.95. ISBN 0-89994-311-X.
Subject: Global economic, ecological, and technological systems.

This book contains three major sections of activities. The first section is a series of six "mini-lesson" warm-up exercises; the second, a section of activities that involve students with the methods that futurists use to make decisions; and the third, activities addressing future issues. Students look at global communication, population, energy resources, food and hunger, future shelter, and so on.

Hunger Project. **Ending Hunger: An Idea Whose Time Has Come.**
New York: Praeger, 1985.
448p. $19.95. ISBN 0-03-006189-X.
Subject: Development issues; human rights; environmental problems.

This publication is designed as a comprehensive sourcebook on world hunger. Its goal is to educate and motivate people to help eliminate world hunger by the year 2000. To this end, the book contains differing perspectives on population, foreign aid, the new international economic order, and other issues central to the problem of world hunger. Extensive color photographs and a timeline of progress to date in ending hunger are included.

Hursh, Heidi, and Michael Prevedel. **Activities Using the New State of the World Atlas.**
Denver, CO: Center for Teaching International Relations, 1988 (rev.).
183p. $21.95. ISBN 0-943804-56-6.
Subject: Global systems and problems.

Designed for use with *The New State of the World Atlas,* this book contains a variety of high-interest activities to help students understand a variety of concepts and issues related to international relations. Students also develop map skills as they interpret various theme maps and data.

Indiana in the World.
Indianapolis: Indiana Department of Public Instruction, 1981.
80p. $5.
Subject: Global economic and technological systems; human values.

This activity book can serve as a prototype for lessons tying a particular state or community to the rest of the world. Adaptable lessons focusing on state multinational corporations in the world, local businesses involved in international trade, ethnic restaurants in a town, and tracing a family tree help students recognize the extensive and varied connections they have with people around the world.

International Trade and Protectionism.
Stanford, CA: Stanford Program on International and Cross-Cultural Education, no date.
77p. $13.95.
Subject: Global political systems; global economic systems.

Students explore international trade issues, with a special focus on the economic relationship between the United States and Taiwan. Major concepts taught include interdependence, free trade, and protectionism. Students culminate the unit with a simulation and role play focused on the U.S.-Taiwan textile trade.

International Trade: U.S./U.S.S.R.
Los Angeles, CA: Constitutional Rights Foundation, 1983.
38p. $4.95.
Subject: Global political systems; global economic systems.

A "business issues mini-unit," this supplementary program helps students understand both political and economic issues separating East and West. Students are involved in a map exercise, case studies, newspaper analysis, and a role play to consider whether the United States should impose sanctions against firms that sell equipment to the Soviet Union.

An Introduction to International Trade: Focus on Japan and the United States.
Stanford, CA: Stanford Program on International and Cross-Cultural Education, 1987.
95p. $12.95.
Subject: Global economic systems; development issues.

A series of activities introduces students to international trade issues that affect their lives. Students examine motives for international trade, effects of trade, economic interdependence, and government trade policies. Several activities focus specifically on trade issues between the United States and Japan.

Johnson, Jacquelyn, John Benegar, and Laurel Singleton. **Global Issues in the Intermediate Classroom.**
Boulder, CO: Social Science Education Consortium, 1989 (rev.).
180p. $21.95. ISBN 0-99994-323-3.
Subject: Global systems and issues.

The lessons in this volume are designed to help students understand and appreciate their own connections to global issues. Activities focus on connections among young people, families, communities, and the global community. The three sections of the book contain activities on global awareness, global interdependence, and cross-cultural understanding. All student and teacher materials are included.

King, David, et al. **Energy Education.** *Intercom 98.*
New York: Global Perspectives in Education, 1980.
32p. $3.50.
Subject: Global ecological systems; global environmental issues.

This issue of the periodical *Intercom* contains case studies, readings, and classroom activities exploring both local and global implications of energy resources and energy shortages.

Koranski, Bruce, ed. **Teaching About the Consumer and the Global Marketplace.**
Denver, CO: Center for Teaching International Relations, 1985.
211p. $21.95. ISBN 0-943804-17-5.
Subject: Global economic systems.

These 31 activities can be used with students in grades 4–12. The activities provide an introduction to the complex link between personal and global economics. Consumer issues are addressed from the following perspectives: (1) the individual as consumer; (2) the government as consumer; (3) the consumer: past, present, and future; and (4) the consumer and the world.

Lamy, Steven L., et al. **Teaching Global Awareness Using the Media.**
Denver, CO: Center for Teaching International Relations, 1985 (rev.).
157p. $21.95. ISBN 0-943804-16-7.
Subject: Global political, economic, and technological systems.

The media's influence is worldwide, touching people in developing as well as industrialized countries. This publication teaches global issues using the media as a focal point. Students participate in 15 activities in which they explore the strategies and impact of print media, radio and television, and advertising.

Larson, James F. **Global Television and Foreign Policy.**
New York: Foreign Policy Association, 1988.
72p. $4. ISBN 0-87124-117-X.
Subject: Global political systems; global technological systems.

Part of the "Headline Series," this book provides an excellent introduction to the role of television media in delivering the news and influencing foreign policy development and administration.

"Law Around the World." *Update on Law-Related Education* 3 no. 4 (Fall 1980).
73p. $2.
Subject: Human values; human rights; global political systems.

This focus issue of the journal *Update on Law-Related Education* contains background articles for teachers as well as classroom activities for a wide range of grade levels. Students look at legal traditions around the world through folklore, alternative methods of dispute resolution in different societies, and the Russian court system. Student handouts are provided.

Mans, Lori, and William Stapp. **Thinking Globally and Acting Locally: Environmental Education Teaching Activities.**
Columbus, OH: ERIC Clearinghouse for Science Education, 1982.
315p. ED 229 214. Available in microfiche ($.75) or paper copy ($23.40) plus postage from the ERIC Document Reproduction Service.
Subject: Global ecological systems; environmental problems.

Activities on food production and distribution, energy, solid waste management, resource management, pollution, and endangered species help learners better understand the relationships between their actions and the world environment. The focus is on cultural linkages and the interdependencies among the nations of the world and between peoples and systems.

McCuen, Gary E., ed. **World Hunger and Social Justice** (Ideas in Conflict Series).
Hudson, WI: Gary McCuen Publications, 1985.
176p. $11.95. ISBN 0-86596-055-0.
Subject: Human values; human rights; development issues.

The realities of world hunger and its relationship to political, economic, and social justice are examined in this book of readings that can be used with high school students. A magazine and book bibliography is provided.

Melnick, Rob, and Hudson Institute staff. **Visions of the Future.**
Pelham Manor, NY: International Center for the Development of Thinking Skills, 1984.
144p. $9.95.
Subject: Global political, economic, and technological systems.

Designed as a supplemental text for a senior high unit on the future, this publication introduces social studies students to perspectives on the future as well as to roles that citizens can play to influence the future. The text covers three areas: (1) exploration of global issues, (2) development of critical thinking skills, and (3) development of a realistic context in which to view the future. Lessons cover such topics as technology, population, future resources, and careers.

Moving Toward A Global Perspective: Social Studies and Second Languages. *Intercom 104.*
New York: Global Perspectives in Education, 1983.
40p. $7.
Subject: Human values.

This issue of the periodical *Intercom* contains both teacher and student materials. Teachers are presented with a rationale for team and interdisciplinary approaches in the teaching of foreign cultures and languages. Eight classroom lessons are provided as models for incorporating global understanding into language-culture lessons. The lessons are organized around the strategies of global skills, cultural universals, and global concepts.

Of Codes and Crowns: The Development of Law.
Los Angeles, CA: Constitutional Rights Foundation, 1983.
Student booklet, 48p, and instructor's manual, 96p. $15.

Subject: Global history; human values; human rights.

A supplement suitable for the study of world history, this program contains lessons on law in early Greece, the ancient Near East, medieval England, and Renaissance Italy. Activities include simulations, role plays, and inquiry lessons. The instructor's manual provides complete background and procedures for conducting all activities.

Shiman, David, et al. **Teaching About Human Rights. Issues of Justice in a Global Age.**
Denver, CO: Center for Teaching International Relations, 1987.
220p. $21.95. ISBN 0-0943804-61-2.
Subject: Human rights; human values.

Using the framework provided by the Universal Declaration of Human Rights, the activities in this book focus on political, economic, civil, and social rights. Sample activities investigate political freedoms across cultures, the quality of life across cultures, the holocaust, human rights and foreign policy, the right to have children, and the death penalty.

Soley, Mary E., Jacquelyn S. Johnson, and Barbara Miller. **Teacher's Resource Guide. Lessons on Current U.S. Foreign Policy Issues for Secondary Social Studies Courses.**
New York: Foreign Policy Association, 1987.
400p. $19.95. ISBN 0-87124-115-3.
Subject: Global political and economic systems; global history.

A total of 17 lessons are designed to help students make connections between history and current events, and to tie these events to the democratic process. Lessons focus on how foreign policy is made, U.S. priorities in foreign policy, the media and foreign policy, terrorism and foreign policy, trade policy, the role of ambassadors in administering foreign policy, and U.S. relations with South Africa, Mexico, Japan, and the Soviet Union. Student handouts, evaluation suggestions, and additional resources are all included.

Survival and Afterward.
Stanford, CA: Stanford Program on International and Cross-Cultural Education, 1987.
80p. $10.95.
Subject: Global technological systems; peace and security issues.

This interdisciplinary social studies–language arts unit helps students explore issues of war and peace in the literature of different cultures. Students also examine the relationship between the treatment of war and peace in ancient and modern literature.

Switzer, Kenneth A., Paul Mulloy, and Karen Smith. **Global Issues. Activities and Resources for the High School Teacher.**
Boulder, CO: Social Science Education Consortium and Center for Teaching International Relations, 1987 (rev.).
122p. $21.95. ISBN 0-89994-312-8.
Subject: Global systems and issues.

This introductory volume provides a wide range of activities to help high school teachers integrate a global perspective into their existing courses. Activities focus on international trade, the arms race, economic development and foreign aid, energy and the environment, and technology. Background, lesson plans, and student handouts are provided.

U.S. Foreign Policy from a Cartoon View.
Mt. Dora, FL: Documentary Photo Aids, no date.
52 photos. $54.50.
Subject: Global political systems; peace and security issues.

Political cartoons by noted cartoonists such as Herblock, Mauldin, and Bishop provide perspective and commentary on the role of the United States in world affairs. Some cartoons go as far back as the American Revolution, but the emphasis is on U.S. foreign policy from 1860 to the present. Sample topics are World War II, Adolf Hitler, the Vietnam War, and nuclear warfare.

U.S.-Mexico Interdependence.
Stanford, CA: Stanford Program on International and Cross-Cultural Education, no date.
44p. $9.95.
Subject: Global economic systems.

This unit introduces secondary students to contemporary issues of international trade and finance by focusing on economic relations between the United States and one of its closest neighbors, Mexico. Students assume roles to analyze a variety of perspectives on the issues, then debate the idea of offshore assembly plants and address the international trade problems raised by monetary devaluation in one nation.

War or Peace in the Twentieth Century.
St. Paul, MN: Greenhaven Press, 1984.
200p. $49.95. ISBN 0-89908-502-4.
Subject: Global political systems; peace and security issues.

This volume focuses student attention on 11 actual international conflicts to help students analyze the factors, moral dilemmas, and competing arguments in potential war situations. For each of the situations, students formulate their own solutions to the problem. Primary source documents for each situation are an integral part of the decision-making exercise.

The World Economy and Multinational Corporations: An Activity Program for Grades 9-12.
Peoria, IL: Caterpillar Tractor Company, 1981.
32p. ED 195 481. Available in microfiche ($.75) or paper copy ($3.60) from the ERIC Document Reproduction Service.
Subject: Global economic systems; development issues.

This booklet, intended for secondary students, contains background information and activities about multinational corporations. Students complete brief reading assignments and participate in a wide variety of classroom activities.

Woyach, Robert, ed. **Bringing a Global Perspective to Economics.**
Columbus, OH: Mershon Center of The Ohio State University, 1983.
118p. $7.50. Available from Social Studies School Service, 10200 Jefferson Blvd., P.O. Box 802, Culver City, CA 90232-0802.
Subject: Global economic systems.

Part of the five-volume Bringing a Global Perspective series, this volume contains lessons designed to add a global dimension to topics usually dealt with in high school economics courses: global food production, foreign investment, multinational corporations, international cartels, trade, and interdependence.

Woyach, Robert, ed. **Bringing a Global Perspective to World History.**
Columbus, OH: Mershon Center of The Ohio State University, 1983.
112p. $7.50. Available from Social Studies School Service, 10200 Jefferson Blvd., P.O. Box 802, Culver City, CA 90232-0802.
Subject: Global history.

Part of the five-volume Bringing a Global Perspective series, this volume adds a global dimension to topics typically covered in a high school world history course. Included are lessons using a global perspective to explore such topics as national heroes, the impact of industrialization and urbanization, foreign policies for peace, and interaction among different cultures.

Woyach, Robert. **World Regions. The Local Connection.**
Columbus, OH: The Columbus Council on World Affairs, 1984.
447p. $7.50.
Subject: Global economic, ecological, and technological systems.

This volume of activities, lessons, and resources helps teach about connections between a U.S. community, state, or region and the rest of the world. Five units within the publication focus on connections with each region of the world. Some lessons—such as proverbs, folklore, foods, and games—are applicable in any class. Other activities are more specific to

Columbus, Ohio, the community for which this publication was developed. However, these lessons are easily adaptable to the characteristics of other communities and offer excellent models.

Zola, John, and Reny Sieck. **Teaching About Conflict, Nuclear War, and the Future.**
Denver, CO: Center for Teaching International Relations, 1984.
219p. $21.95. ISBN 0-943804-55-8.
Subject: Peace and security issues; human values.

This publication contains 25 activities to help students foster an appreciation of alternative solutions to global conflict. Students learn conflict management concepts, the language of conflict, and the application of theories to actual international conflict situations. An extensive bibliography is provided for the teacher.

Zola, John, and Jaye Zola. **Teaching About Peace and Nuclear War. A Balanced Approach.**
Boulder, CO: Social Science Education Consortium and Center for Teaching International Relations, 1985.
109p. $10.95. ISBN 0-89994-305-5.
Subject: Peace and security issues.

This handbook for teachers provides a rationale and definition of peace and nuclear war education and examines how teachers can responsibly teach about these and other controversial issues. A system for evaluating classroom materials on the topic is provided.

Textbooks

Abramowitz, Jack. **World History for a Global Age.**
New York: Globe Books, 1985.
2 vol., 250p and 282p. $16.20. (A teacher's guide is also available.) Volume 1, ISBN 0-87065-648-1; Volume 2, ISBN 0-87065-646-5.

This two-volume, softbound text is intended for a year-long course in world history for below-average high school readers. The text is ordered chronologically and topically, considering Western and non-Western cultures within each time span. Global concepts and themes are infused throughout the program, helping students recognize and appreciate the inter-connectedness of peoples and cultures. The text also places a heavy emphasis on skill development. Volume 1 covers world history to the nineteenth century; volume 2 continues the chronology to contemporary

times. The text treats cultural and technological history as well as the
standard political-military history.

Backler, Alan, and Robert Hanvey. **Global Geography.**
New York: Teacher's College Press, 1986.
396p. $15.95. (A teacher's manual is also available.) ISBN 0-8077-6103-6.

This text alternates chapters on the world's regions with chapters on basic
geographic concepts. Focus is on helping students see the connections
between regions and events while developing geographic skills and
knowledge. The text features case studies, primary readings, map activities,
and skills-building exercises.

Backler, Alan, and Stuart Lazarus. **World Geography.**
Evanston, IL: McDougal, Littell and Company, 1986 (rev.).
*596p. $22.47. (An instructor's manual and student workbook are available.)
ISBN 0-86609-146-7.*

Each of five units within this text focuses on a fundamental theme of
geography: location, physical and human characteristics, relationships within
and between places, human interaction with the environment, and location
and place.

Christensen, John. **Global Science: Energy, Resources, Environment.** 2d ed.
Dubuque, IA: Kendall/Hunt Publishing Company, 1984.
355p. $19.95. ISBN 0-8403-3389-7.

Designed as a basal textbook for a global science course, this publication
contains ten units, which present the following concepts in global
perspective: the ecosystem; energy and resources; growth, population, and
food; energy supply and demand; energy for the future; mineral resources;
making peace with the environment; the economics of resources and the
environment; energy and society as a concept; and the future. The text may
also form the core of an earth studies or physical science course.

Farah, Mounir, et al. **The Human Experience: A World History.**
Columbus, OH: Charles E. Merrill Publishing Company, 1985.
*830p. $21.90. (A complete program set includes a teacher's annotated edition,
activity book, teacher's annotated activity book, and loose-leaf teacher's
resource book.) ISBN 0-675-022271-1.*

This text offers material for a year-long course in world history from
a global perspective. Both Western and non-Western history are given
coverage. It uses a chronological approach and includes special features
on cities, science and technology, the arts, and people.

Global Issues 87/88. Annual Editions Series.
Guilford, CT: Dushkin Publishers, 1987.
256p. $9.95. ISBN 0-87967-733-3.

This text can be used with students in grades 11–12. It contains a collection of 52 articles and essays examining major global issues and trends. The articles address such topics as the global environment, development among industrial and nonindustrial nations, human rights and values, and conflict areas. Used collectively, the articles can form the basis of a contemporary global issues or global studies course.

Global Studies Series.
Guilford, CT: Dushkin Publishers, 1986–1987.

Components are:

    Latin America. 212p. $9.95. ISBN 0-87967-619-1.

    Africa. 256p. $9.95. ISBN 0-87967-690-6.

    Soviet Union and Eastern Europe. 212p. $9.95. ISBN 0-87967-561-6.

    China. 176p. $9.95. ISBN 0-87967-691-4.

    Middle East. 212p. $9.95. ISBN 0-87967-610-8.

Taken together, this series of five paperback volumes provides a comprehensive study of the world's regions and nations: Africa, China, Latin America, the Middle East, and the Soviet Union and Eastern Europe. Each volume begins with an essay portraying similarities and differences among nations within the given region. A brief overview of each nation is provided, as well as maps, charts, graphs, recent articles from the world press, and other information.

Hantula, James Neil, et al. **Global Insights.**
Columbus, OH: Merrill Publishing Company, 1987.
912p. $22.95. (A teacher's guide and teacher's resource book are also available.) ISBN 0-675-02004-2.

This world cultures text contains comprehensive units on Africa, China, Japan, India, Latin America, the Middle East, the Soviet Union, and Western Europe. Each unit provides a chapter on geography, a chapter or more of historical overview, a chapter on art and culture, and a chapter on daily life. Continent units also include several chapters that are case studies of specific countries. Although interrelations among countries and regions are not explicit, the coverage of each region is thorough and detailed.

Leone, Bruno, ed. **The Isms: Modern Doctrines and Movements.**
St. Paul, MN: Greenhaven Press, Inc., 1986.

Components are:
  Internationalism. 176p. $7.95.
  Racism. 233p. $7.95.
  Socialism. 156p. $7.95.
  Nationalism. 145p. $7.95.
  Capitalism. 168p. $7.95.
  Communism. 216p. $7.95.
  Feminism. 261p. $7.95.

Part of Greenhaven Press's Opposing Viewpoints series, each of the seven volumes in this set contains anthologies of pro and con positions on a critical ideology of the contemporary world. Writings of key philosophers and political thinkers are provided in primary source materials.

Peoples and Cultures Series.
Evanston, IL: McDougal, Littell, 1982–83.
94–166p. Set of 9 paperbacks, $64.

This nine-volume series may constitute a textbook for area studies, world history, or world culture classes at the high school level. Each volume employs primary source material. Titles in the series are *Learning About Peoples and Cultures, Africa, The Soviet Union, Southeast Asia, The Mediterranean Rim, China, India, Japan,* and *Latin America.*

Roselle, Daniel. **Our Common Heritage: A World History.**
Lexington, MA: Ginn and Company, 1984 (rev.).
678p. $16.95. (A teacher's guide is also available.) ISBN 0-663-41729-5.

This textbook places heavy emphasis on non-Western cultures in its coverage of world history from ancient to modern times. Coverage of artistic and scientific developments throughout history in different cultures and countries is also emphasized. The text is appropriate for a year-long course in world history at the high school level.

Rosenfeld, Erwin, and Harriet Geller. **Global Studies: Volume One.**
Woodbury, NY: Barron's, 1987.
632p. $16.95.

This is a comprehensive social studies text that covers Africa, Asia, the Middle East, and Latin America. Each region is covered in a separate unit.

Wallbank, T. Walter, et al. **History and Life: The World and Its People.**
Glenview, IL: Scott, Foresman and Company, 1987 (rev.).
798p. $25.40. (The complete program includes a teacher's annotated text, a student activity book, teacher's edition of the activity book, a loose-leaf teacher resource book, and a test generator package.) ISBN 0-673-22261-6.

This world history text is organized chronologically, considering different geographic and cultural areas during each time period. The text provides an extensive and well-balanced treatment of non-Western history as well as the traditional coverage of Western civilization. Coverage includes political and military history as well as economic, social, and intellectual history.

Welty, Paul Thomas. **The Human Expression: A History of the World.**
New York: Harper and Row, 1985 (rev.).
854p. $17.28. (A teacher's manual, student workbook, and teacher's edition of the workbook are also available.) ISBN 0-06-554301-7.

Designed for a year-long course in world history, this is a comprehensive, interdisciplinary text. Following an introductory section on the study of culture, the text is divided into five sections, which cover ancient through modern history in each of the following culture areas: the Middle East, Asia, Africa, Western Europe, Eastern Europe and the Soviet Union, and Latin America. Coverage of global issues is integrated into appropriate units throughout the text.

Videocassettes and Films

Africa: A Voyage of Discovery with Basil Davidson

Subject: Development
Type: Color videocassettes: VHS
Grades: 9–12
Length: Eight 57-min. segments (2 per videocassette)
Buy/rent: $69.95 per 2-segment videocassette/no rental
Source: Social Studies School Service (distributor)
    10200 Jefferson Blvd.
    P.O. Box 802
    Culver City, CA 90232-0802
Date: 1984

These videocassettes present a comprehensive overview of African history, geography, and culture from ancient times to the present. Titles in the two-cassette segments include "Different but Equal" and "Mastering a Continent," "Caravans of Gold" and "Kings and Cities," "The Bible and the Gun" and "This Magnificent African Cake," and "The Rise of Nationalism" and "The Legacy."

Around South America

Subject: Development; environment
Type: Color videocassette: VHS
Grades: 7–12
Length: 57 min.
Buy/rent: $39.95/no rental
Source: Social Studies School Service (distributor)
             10200 Jefferson Blvd.
             P.O. Box 802
             Culver City, CA 90232-0802
Date: 1987

The richness of the South American continent is highlighted in this travelog-format video. The scope of Latin American history and geography is illustrated by visits to major cities and landforms.

The Atomic Cafe

Subject: Peace; security
Type: Color and black-and-white videocassette:VHS
Grades: 9–12
Length: 92 min.
Buy/rent: $68.50/no rental
Source: Social Studies School Service (distributor)
             10200 Jefferson Blvd.
             P.O. Box 802
             Culver City, CA 90232-0802
Date: No date given

Clips of documentaries, TV shows, newsreels, cartoons, and training films are combined to show how Americans perceived "the bomb" in the forties and fifties.

China: World of Difference

Subject: Development
Type: Color videocassette: VHS
Grades: 7–12
Length: 50 min.
Buy/rent: $24.95/no rental
Source: Social Studies School Service (distributor)
             10200 Jefferson Blvd.
             P.O. Box 802
             Culver City, CA 90232-0802
Date: No date given

The daily life of China is illustrated in this tour of the nation. Stops include Shanghai, Soochow, the Great Wall, the Forbidden City, and the Ming Tombs.

Conquest

Subject:	Technology; peace and security
Type:	Color videocassette: VHS
Grades:	9-12
Length:	180 min.
Buy/rent:	$59.95/no rental
Source:	Social Studies School Service (distributor)
	10200 Jefferson Blvd.
	P.O. Box 802
	Culver City, CA 90232-0802
Date:	No date given

A comprehensive history of space exploration is detailed in this videocassette. The program concludes with speculations on the future of space exploration.

Cross-Cultural Studies

Subject:	Development; environment; technology; economic systems
Type:	Color filmstrips on videocassettes: VHS, Beta
Grades:	7-12
Length:	Each videocassette varies from 30 to 49 min.
Buy/rent:	$79 per videocassette; $299.50 for complete series of 4 videocassettes/no rental
Source:	Social Studies School Service (distributor)
	10200 Jefferson Blvd.
	P.O. Box 802
	Culver City, CA 90232-0802
Date:	1987

The cultural traits of people around the world are explored in this recently revised four-part series. The daily lives and living conditions, ceremonies, customs, and other aspects of culture are examined. Series titles include *Family, Clothing, Food,* and *Housing.*

East-West Relations: Competition or Cooperation?

Subject:	Development; peace and security
Type:	Color videocassette: VHS
Grades:	10-12
Length:	53 min.
Buy/rent:	$69/no rental
Source:	Close Up Foundation
	Publications Department
	1235 Jefferson Davis Highway
	Arlington, VA 22202
Date:	1987

Originally produced for C-SPAN television, this panel discussion format video covers several questions of importance to current international development and cooperation. Can the East and West work together on the problems of apartheid or the ozone layer? How can the United States criticize the Soviet Union's actions in Afghanistan when the United States supports dictatorships in Central America?

Economic Geography: Comparing Two Nations

Subject: Development
Type: Color videocassette: VHS, Beta, ¾" U-Matic; or 16mm film
Grades: 7–12
Length: 11 min.
Buy/rent: Videocassette: $135/$33 for day one, $16.50 for each day
           thereafter
           16mm film: $220/$33 for day one, $16.50 for each day
           thereafter
Source: BFA Educational Media
           468 Park Avenue South
           New York, NY 10016
Date: 1971

This program looks at two nations, examining why one succeeds economically whereas the second, with similar resources, remains underdeveloped.

Economic Geography: Three Families in Different Environments

Subject: Development; environment
Type: Color videocassette: VHS, Beta; or 16mm color film
Grades: 7–9
Length: 15 min.
Buy/rent: Videocassette: $195/$46 for day one, $23 for each day thereafter
           16mm film: $250/$46 for day one, $23 for each day thereafter
Source: BFA Educational Media
           468 Park Avenue South
           New York, NY 10016
Date: 1971

Students learn about three families: (1) the rainforest family that lives directly off the land; (2) a U.S. farm family that lives partially off the land, but also grows and sells some crops to buy some goods; and (3) a city family that takes almost nothing from the land, and instead relies upon wages paid for specialized work.

E. F. Schumacher . . . As If People Mattered

Subject: Development
Type: Color videocassette: VHS, Beta, ¾" U-Matic; or 16mm color film

Grades: 7–12
Length: 16 min.
Buy/rent: VHS or Beta: $70/$30
            ¾" U-Matic: $80/$30
            16mm film: $315/$30
Source: Bullfrog Films, Inc.
            Oley, PA 19547
Date: 1979

Schumacher shows how the resource-rich state of Montana is an example of what he calls "internal colonization," i.e., the development of parts of countries, not for their own sake, but to serve the needs of large commercial and industrial centers. Once the needed resource is spent, the rural population is left resentful.

Europe Since World War II
Subject: Political; economic; development; peace and security
Type: Black-and-white videocassette: VHS
Grades: 7–12
Length: 42 min.
Buy/rent: $189/no rental
Source: Social Studies School Service (distributor)
            10200 Jefferson Blvd.
            P.O. Box 802
            Culver City, CA 90232-0802
Date: 1986

Using documentary footage to illustrate the devastation of Europe following the war, this videocassette shows how various countries recovered. The production discusses Europe's loss of power to the United States and the Soviet Union, Western Europe's attempts to unify, and Eastern Europe's political unrest and improvements in living conditions.

The Global Community: A Unit of Study
Subject: Political; economic; technology; peace and security; development; environment; human rights
Type: Color filmstrips on videocassettes: VHS
Grades: 7–12
Length: No times given
Buy/rent: $145/no rental
Source: Social Studies School Service (distributor)
            10200 Jefferson Blvd.
            P.O. Box 802
            Culver City, CA 90232-0802
Date: 1985

Global interdependence, its characteristics, and positive and negative effects are explored in this series of filmstrips on videocassette. Titles include*Global Interdependence—What Is It?*, *Global Interdependence—Its Consequences*, *Population and Food Issues*, and *Geopolitical and Resources Issues*. Student exercises are provided on reproducible handouts.

Hunger: Whose Problem Is It?

Subject: Development; environment
Type: Color videocassette: VHS, Beta, ¾″ U-Matic
Grades: 9–12
Length: 60 min.
Buy/rent: $90/$50
Source: Close Up Foundation
Publications Department
1235 Jefferson Davis Highway
Arlington, VA 22202
Date: 1986

The cause and effects of world hunger are discussed in this teleconference with high school students, key government officials, and experts in the area. Ongoing efforts to solve the worldwide problem of hunger are also discussed.

International Human Rights

Subject: Human rights
Type: Color videocassette: VHS
Grades: 10–12
Length: 60 min.
Buy/rent: $59/no rental
Source: Close Up Foundation
Publications Department
1235 Jefferson Davis Highway
Arlington, VA 22202
Date: 1986

The executive director of Amnesty International USA answers questions from a group of social studies teachers about the state of human rights around the world. Also discussed are the policies and operations of Amnesty International.

International Trade

Subject: Development; environment
Type: Color videocassette: VHS, Beta, ¾″ U-Matic
Grades: 9–12
Length: 60 min.
Buy/rent: $90/$50

Source: Close Up Foundation
            Publications Department
            1235 Jefferson Davis Highway
            Arlington, VA 22202
Date: 1985

High school students question an expert and a senator on aspects of
international trade. Topics include trade deficits, tariffs, interest rates,
protectionism, and import quotas.

International Trade: America's Vital Economic Interest

Subject: Development
Type: Color videocassette: VHS, Beta, ¾" U-Matic
Grades: 9–12
Length: 30 min.
Buy/rent: $75/$35
Source: Close Up Foundation
            Publications Department
            1235 Jefferson Davis Highway
            Arlington, VA 22202
Date: 1984

Economic experts explain how worldwide economic strength is affected
daily by the trading policies and fiscal well-being of each country that
participates in international trade. Topics discussed include the value of
the dollar, the U.S. budget deficit, interest rates, protectionist legislation,
unemployment, and the use of economic sanctions to achieve political goals.

The Middle East and U.S. Foreign Policy

Subject: Peace and security; development; environment
Type: Color videocassette: VHS
Grades: 10–12
Length: 30 min.
Buy/rent: $59/no rental
Source: Social Studies School Service (distributor)
            10200 Jefferson Blvd.
            P.O. Box 802
            Culver City, CA 90232-0802
Date: 1985

U.S. students question Middle East experts on the problems facing the
United States in its relations with the Middle East. Topics covered include
sales of weapons to the Middle East, the PLO, and the Iran-Iraq war.

Miniature Miracle

Subject: Technology
Type: Color videocassette: VHS
Grades: 7-12
Length: 60 min.
Buy/rent: $35.50/no rental
Source: National Geographic Society
               Education Services
               Dept. 88
               Washington, DC 20036
Date: 1985

The development of the microchip and the subsequent advances in computers, medicine, aviation, and art are explored in this video.

Nigeria

Subject: Development
Type: Color videocassette: VHS
Grades: 6-12
Length: 20 min.
Buy/rent: $35/no rental
               Spiralbound reproducible activity book: $12
Source: Social Studies School Service (distributor)
               10200 Jefferson Blvd.
               P.O. Box 802
               Culver City, CA 90232-0802
Date: No date given

The interactions of traditional and modern life are highlighted in this program on the changes in Nigerian society since independence. Topics include agriculture, natural resources, people, history, religions, and education.

Nuclear Weapons: Concepts and Controversies

Subject: Peace and security
Type: Color videocassette: VHS
Grades: 10-12
Length: No times given
Buy/rent: $139/no rental
Source: Social Studies School Service (distributor)
               10200 Jefferson Blvd.
               P.O. Box 802
               Culver City, CA 90232-0802
Date: 1985

After tracing the development of nuclear weapons, this program examines how their existence has changed military strategy, foreign policy, and international relations. Part 1 distinguishes nuclear from conventional weapons; part 2 illustrates the evolution of military strategies in the face of technological developments.

On Common Ground: A Tour of the United Nations

Subject: Political; economic; technology; peace and security; development; environment; human rights
Type: Color and black-and-white videocassette: VHS
Grades: 7–12
Length: 30 min.
Buy/rent: $22.95/no rental
Source: Social Studies School Service (distributor)
10200 Jefferson Blvd.
P.O. Box 802
Culver City, CA 90232-0802
Date: 1987

A tour of the United Nations building takes viewers behind the scenes to examine the goals and origins of the institution. Documentary footage is interspersed to illustrate the work of the various agencies around the world.

The Other Nuclear Arms Race

Subject: Peace and security; technology; political
Type: Color videocassette: VHS
Grades: 10–12
Length: 30 min.
Buy/rent: $139/no rental
Source: Social Studies School Service (distributor)
10200 Jefferson Blvd.
P.O. Box 802
Culver City, CA 90232-0802
Date: 1986

Several noted experts comment on the "other" arms race—nuclear proliferation. The topics of nuclear terrorism and arms control treaties are discussed.

Political Ideologies of the Twentieth Century

Subject: Political; economic
Type: Color filmstrips on videocassettes: VHS
Grades: 10–12
Length: No time given
Buy/rent: $139 for each of 6 videocassettes/no rental
Complete set: $768

Source: Social Studies School Service (distributor)
             10200 Jefferson Blvd.
             P.O. Box 802
             Culver City, CA 90232-0802
Date: No date given

The characteristics, advantages and disadvantages, and development of the entire range of political and economic systems of the twentieth century are explored in this six-part series. The segments include *What Is Socialism?*, *What Is Facism?*, *What Is Capitalism?*, *What Is Communism?*, *Comparative Political Systems: The United States, The United Kingdom and the Soviet Union*; and *Liberalism/Conservatism.*

Soviet Military Power—1987

Subject: Peace and security; technology
Type: Color videocassette: VHS
Grades: 10–12
Length: 25 min.
Buy/rent: $110/no rental
Source: Social Studies School Service (distributor)
              10200 Jefferson Blvd.
              P.O. Box 802
              Culver City, CA 90232-0802
Date: 1987

This U.S. Department of Defense documentary on the Soviet military is a fast-paced survey of the Soviet arsenal. The sophisticated graphics and photography are accompanied by a 160-page book detailing recent advances in military technology. The program can be used with advanced students to stimulate discussion on the arms race.

Terrorism: Battleground of the '80s

Subject: Peace and security; human rights; development
Type: Color videocassette: VHS
Grades: 10–12
Length: 60 min.
Buy/rent: $59/no rental
Source: Close Up Foundation
              Publications Department
              1235 Jefferson Davis Highway
              Arlington, VA 22202
Date: 1986

Experts on international terrorism respond to the questions of high school students. Questions discussed include: What is terrorism? What are its ends? Who are terrorists? How can we stop it?

The Third World Challenge to U.S. Policy

Subject: Political; economic; technology; peace and security
Type: Color videocassette: VHS
Grades: 10–12
Length: 20 min.
Buy/rent: $50/no rental
Source: Social Studies School Service (distributor)
   10200 Jefferson Blvd.
   P.O. Box 802
   Culver City, CA 90232-0802
Date: 1985

A multilayered approach to the complex problems of North/South relationships is presented in this thought-provoking program. Issues of human rights in conflict with political ideology are carefully explored. A 12-page background pamphlet and a discussion manual with reproducible fact sheets are included.

To Bear Witness

Subject: Peace and security; human rights
Type: Color and black-and-white videocassette: VHS
Grades: 10–12
Length: 41 min.
Buy/rent: $140/no rental
Source: Social Studies School Service (distributor)
   10200 Jefferson Blvd.
   P.O. Box 802
   Culver City, CA 90232-0802
Date: 1981

This production captures testimony from the First International Liberators conference in 1981. Testimony of survivors and liberators of Nazi concentration camps is interspersed with documentary footage. Audiences will need some preparation before viewing the graphic violence of the camps.

U.S./Soviet Relations

Subject: Development; peace and security
Type: Color videocassette: VHS, Beta, ¾″ U-Matic
Grades: 10–12
Length: 120 min.
Buy/rent: VHS: $199/no rental
   Beta: $199/no rental
   ¾″ U-Matic: $199/no rental

Source: Close Up Foundation
             Publications Department
             1235 Jefferson Davis Highway
             Arlington, VA 22202
Date: 1986

This series of four 30-minute color video segments examines the complex
relationship between the two superpowers. Each segment begins with a 12-
minute documentary followed by a question-and-answer session where high
school students question U.S. experts on the Soviet Union. The segment titles
are *Differing World Views; The Evolution of U.S./Soviet Relations; A Critical
Issue: The Arms Race; U.S./Soviet Relations: In Pursuit of Peace.*

Video from Russia: The People Speak
Subject: Peace and security
Type: Color videocassette: VHS
Grades: 9–12
Length: 30 min.
Buy/rent: $29.95/no rental
Source: Social Studies School Service (distributor)
             10200 Jefferson Blvd.
             P.O. Box 802
             Culver City, CA 90232-0802
Date: 1984

Two U.S. journalists interview people on the streets of various cities
throughout the Soviet Union without the permission of the Soviet authorities.
A candid portrait of the Soviet people emerges.

World Poverty and Foreign Aid
Subject: Development; human rights; economic; political; technology
Type: Color videocassette: VHS
Grades: 10–12
Length: 59 min.
Buy/rent: $69/no rental
Source: Social Studies School Service (distributor)
             10200 Jefferson Blvd.
             P.O. Box 802
             Culver City, CA 90232-0802
Date: 1987

This question-and-answer session explores problems and concerns in the
conflicts between political systems and the need to feed the hungry of the
world.

World Poverty and U.S. Foreign Aid

Subject: Development
Type: Color videocassette: VHS, Beta, ¾″ U-Matic
Grades: 9–12
Length: 30 min.
Buy/rent: $75/$35
Source: Close Up Foundation
              Publications Department
              1235 Jefferson Davis Highway
              Arlington, VA 22202
Date: 1985

The topic of the responsibilities of the United States with regard to providing aid to foreign countries is discussed among students and experts in the area. Specific topics include the effective distribution of foreign aid, the long-term outlook for countries receiving U.S. aid, and the need to aid poverty-stricken U.S. citizens.

Glossary of Terms

absolutism   A type of government in which the authority and power of the heads of state are not effectively limited by a constitution or other laws.

acculturation   The process whereby new cultural traits are adopted into an existing culture, or the process of the mutual modification of two or more different cultures in contact with each other.

adjudication   In international law, a decision made in a dispute between two or more parties by a permanent court of law such as the International Court of Justice, located in the Netherlands.

aggression   The use of armed force by a state against the sovereignty, territorial integrity, or political independence of another state.

agrarian movement   A social movement in which the farmers of a nation seek to reorganize the agricultural economy and emphasize the relative importance of agriculture in the total economy of the country while improving their own economic and political status.

alien   A person living in a given nation who was born elsewhere and who is not a citizen of his or her country of residence.

allegiance   The expression of loyalty, support, and confidence in a government.

alliance   A multilateral agreement by states to improve their power position by joining together in defense of their common interests.

ambassador   The top-ranking diplomat sent by the government of a nation as its official representative to another nation.

anarchism   The view that any kind of government or formal administrative control over a society is evil and unnecessary.

anarchy   A hypothetical society without leaders or a government. Also a chaotic political condition or lack of order in a society.

apartheid   In South Africa, the system of institutionalized racial segregation.

appeasement   A term used to describe concessions made to a warlike potential enemy in the hope that further demands will be deferred and the peace will be maintained.

appropriate technology   A technology that uses locally abundant resources in preference to locally scarce resources.

arbitrage   The act of simultaneously buying goods in one market and selling in another, in order to make a profit on the price differences in the two markets.

arbitration   A process by which parties to a dispute agree to submit the issue in question to one or more umpires or judges for a decision that is binding. The judges are selected by the parties to the dispute.

aristocracy   The highest of the social classes. Also, rule or domination by the people of the highest social class.

arms control   Any plan or process that regulates some aspect of the production, numbers, or performance characteristics of weapons systems.

assimilation   The process by which the people of two or more cultures in physical contact lose their unique cultural identities and become fused into a single homogeneous cultural unit that is different from any of the original component cultural units.

assured destructive capability   The ability to destroy without question the society of an enemy with nuclear weapons after receiving an all-out nuclear attack by that enemy.

autarchy   Political sovereignty; self-government; economic self-sufficiency.

authoritarianism   The view that group interests are best achieved and best served through the arbitrary and unlimited exercise of power by the agents of government.

authority   The power associated with an office or official status to give and enforce orders.

autocracy   The rule or domination of others by one person or a small group of people whose powers cannot be legally restricted nor openly disputed by those who are governed.

balance of payments   A summary statement of all the economic transactions between one country and the rest of the world for a one-year period. The term often refers to the difference between a nation's receipts and payments.

balance of power   A situation in which peace and security are maintained through an equilibrium of power between two or more rival nations.

balance of terror   Mutual deterrence from nuclear attack by both the Soviet Union and the United States against the other. Because both nations possess such powerful nuclear weapons neither would emerge a victor.

balance of trade   The difference between the value of the imported and the exported goods of a nation.

bilateral aid   The transfer of funds, goods, and/or services directly from one country to another.

birth rate, crude   The number of live births each year per thousand population. A "crude" rate is the rate computed for an entire population.

black market   Illegal buying or selling that occurs in violation of government restrictions.

bourgeoisie   The merchants, artisans, and other town dwellers that comprise the capitalist class of enterprisers who hire employees. Also the middle classes, regardless of their occupations.

buffer state   A relatively small and weak sovereign state that lies between two more powerful states.

bureaucracy   The organization of major institutional functions in a society into a variety of smaller organizations, each performing a special function that contributes to the accomplishment of the major institutional goals.

bureaucratization   The process of organizing diverse special functions into an administrative hierarchy of functions.

capital   The wealth, in money or property, owned or employed by an individual, firm, or corporation.

capital goods   Goods that are used in production and have themselves been produced for financial capital.

capitalism   An economic system of producing and distributing wealth in which the spirit of the system favors the widespread private ownership of the means of production by individuals or by groups of individuals. Individuals are encouraged to take initiative in business enterprise primarily for private profit and at private risk.

carrying capacity   The maximum size of a resident population that can be sustained in a given ecosystem.

cartel   An international association of independent business enterprisers who have combined to control or dominate some aspect of the production or the international distribution of goods.

cash cropping   Growing crops for sale in the market rather than for family consumption, as in subsistence farming.

census   A periodic count, by systematic visitation, of the total number of people living in a given area at a given time, and a compilation of certain other data about them.

centralization   The concentration of political power in a central government at the expense of the local administrative units.

civilization   A complex society that is controlled by codified laws enforced by civil authority, is literate, uses metals, has a machine technology, and has a money economy.

class   A group of people who have the same status in a given society. Various criteria, such as occupation, amount of property, or income, as well as self-identification, can be used to determine class membership.

collective agriculture   An agricultural system that is organized into farms owned by the state or a collective. The farms are managed by the workers and/or the state.

collective security   A worldwide security system by which all or most nations agree in advance to take collective action against any state or states that break the peace by committing aggression.

colonialism   The system of political and economic administration whereby a dominant country controls and exploits the resources of dominated peoples, who are often of a different culture.

COMECON   The Council for Mutual Economic Assistance. Formed in 1949. its members are Bulgaria, Cuba, Czechoslovakia, East Germany, Hungary, Mongolia, Poland, Romania, and the Soviet Union, with Yugoslavia as an associate member. Its purpose is to coordinate and integrate members' economies, under USSR leadership.

Cominform   Soviet organization designed to direct international Communist party political activities.

Comintern   The Communist International, founded in 1919. It is the predecessor of Cominform and served mainly as a vehicle to promote Soviet interests on a worldwide basis.

command economy   An economic system in which decisions regarding the factors of production are made by government leaders.

communism   A type of socioeconomic system in which ideally there would be no private property, no religion, and no government. All capital would be controlled through common ownership.

constitution   A document of laws that defines the purposes of government and the proper ways of achieving them.

constitutionalism   The political ideology that holds that the executive branch of government should exercise only those powers that have been granted to it in a constitution.

containment   A general policy adopted in 1947 by the Truman administration to build strong military positions around the periphery of the Soviet Union and Eastern Europe in order to contain communism within its existing boundaries.

convergence theory   The view that the capitalist and Communist systems are evolving in their economic functions and operations in increasingly similar ways.

cosmopolitanism   A world outlook that seeks to transcend local loyalties and values.

country of origin   The country from which an emigrant starts on his journey to another country of residence.

creditor nation   A nation that owes less to other nations than they owe to it.

cultural autonomy   The recognized right of any culture group in a multicultural society to preserve its unique cultural identity, and to perpetuate and elaborate its language and customs without interference from other culture groups.

cultural bias   The predisposition to evaluate certain social phenomena in terms of the values of a given culture.

cultural imperialism   The deliberate and calculated process of forcing a cultural minority to adopt the culture of the dominant group in a society.

cultural pluralism   The coexistence of several different cultural groups in a multinational state.

cultural relativism   The point of view in which each cultural group is evaluated in terms of its own value system.

culture   All of the learned socially meaningful conduct practiced in a given society, including, among others, customs; norms; language; religious, economic, and political beliefs and practices; and art.

customs duty   A tax levied on goods coming into a country.

customs union   An economic cooperative arrangement between two or more states that culminates in the elimination of tariff barriers between the member states, and the establishment of a common external tariff imposed on imports from nonmember states.

de facto government The government that is in power and actually functioning as a political unit.

de facto recognition The diplomatic recognition of a state by another state that does not imply a full acceptance of the new state.

de jure government The legally authorized and empowered government that functions in a state.

de jure recognition The full legal recognition of one state by another, wherein there is an exchange of diplomatic representatives.

death rate, crude The number of deaths each year per thousand population. A "crude" rate is the rate computed for an entire population.

democracy A political system in which the mass of the governed has the right and the power to choose their leaders and to determine the general lines of public policy.

demographic transition The transition of population growth rates from a slow-growth stage (with high birth and death rates), through a rapid-growth stage (with high birth rates and low death rates), to a low-growth stage (with low birth and death rates).

demography The quantitative study of the age and sex composition of a population, and the movement of people from place to place.

détente Efforts by the Communist and non-Communist countries of Europe and North America to reduce tensions and to bring about greater economic cooperation, cultural exchanges, and human contacts.

deterrence Dissuasion of a political adversary from initiating an attack or conflict, often by the threat of unacceptable retaliatory damage.

developed countries The industrialized nations.

developing countries Countries in the Third World that are seeking to use their limited resources to develop industries.

development The process of improving the quality of human lives in many areas, including income and consumption levels; social, political, and economic institutions; and freedom of choice.

dialectical materialism A frame of reference based on the following premises: (1) nothing is static or absolute; (2) all change is conflict; (3) economics determines all institutional change; and (4) conflict can be understood only in terms of dialectical reasoning—that is, any norm, practice, or value automatically produces an opposite and conflicting norm or practice. The existing phenomenon and the conflicting phenomenon produce a new phenomenon, which is a synthesis of the two. The synthesis inevitably produces a new conflicting antithetical phenomenon and the process continues.

dictatorship   A political system in which a few have arbitrary power over the masses of people, and are not effectively restrained by any laws, courts, elections, or public opinion.

diffusion   The spreading of cultural traits from one cultural group to another.

diplomacy   The total process by which states carry on political relations with each other.

diplomatic privileges and immunities   Under international law, ambassadors and other diplomatic officials enjoy special rights and are immune from the jurisdiction of the state to which they are assigned. The embassy grounds may not be trespassed upon by local officials unless permission is granted.

disarmament   All measures related to the prevention, limitation, reduction, or elimination of weapons and military forces.

displaced person   A person who was either taken from or voluntarily fled his/her homeland and refuses to return there.

domino theory   The doctrine that assumes if some key nation or geographical region falls into Communist control, a string of other nations will subsequently topple "like a row of dominoes."

dual citizenship   Citizenship in two nations at the same time.

ecology   The study of the reciprocal influences between humans and their physical, or geographic, environment.

economic barrier   Any tariff or quota that restricts trade.

economic determinism   The doctrine that economic factors, such as economic class position, the "profit motive," competition for markets, and so on, are the basic factors in shaping the social, political, religious, educational, and other institutional norms, practices, and beliefs in every society.

economic imperialism   The economic relationship, planned or accidental, between nations wherein an economically advanced nation dominates and arbitrarily controls the economy of another nation.

economic nationalism   An economic policy by which a nation seeks to attain economic prosperity through extensive government control of trade.

economic union Full harmonization of economic policies among the member-states of a regional economic cooperative arrangement such as the European community.

economics The study of everything that is related to the creation of goods and services, the management of the processes of production, the distribution of goods, and the extent and character of the consumption of such goods and services.

economy The predominant type of productive procedure that is followed in a given society.

ecosystem The system of all life forms on earth.

emigrant A person who leaves a country to settle elsewhere permanently.

emigration The act of leaving the country of residence legally and voluntarily establishing residence elsewhere.

ethnocentrism An intolerance of the ways of behaving that differ from those of one's native culture.

ethos The basic character of an ethnic group that makes it distinct from all other ethnic groups.

European community A collective term for three European communities, the European Coal and Steel Community, the European Economic Community, and the European Atomic Energy Community.

executive agreement An international agreement between the president of the United States and foreign heads of state that, unlike treaties, does not require Senate consent.

expatriation The voluntary surrender of citizenship.

exponential growth Growth in which a constant percentage of an expanding whole is added each time period. Also known is a "geometric ratio of growth."

extradition Return by one nation to another of a person accused of a crime.

factors of production Those four elements necessary to produce anything: land, labor, capital, and management.

fertility rate, general The number of live births per thousand women of childbearing age.

fertility rate, replacement level The fertility rate at which women of childbearing age have just enough daughters to replace themselves in the population.

foreign aid   The gift or loan of funds, goods, and/or services from one government to another, either directly or through an intermediary organization.

foreign exchange   All monetary instruments whereby residents of one country hold claims on another. This includes the currency of that country, interest-bearing bonds, and gold.

foreign exchange earnings   Income earned by nations from their exports.

Fourth World   The poorest of the Third World countries.

frame of reference   The points of view, assumptions, hypotheses, preconceptions, evaluations, and thought categories with which a person approaches social phenomena.

free enterprise system   An economic system in which it is relatively easy to start and manage a business without government interference or ownership.

free trade area   An economic cooperation arrangement in which two or more states participate and which culminates in the elimination of all tariff barriers between the participating countries.

functionalism   The process by which the economic and social needs of peoples are successfully met through border-crossing collaboration arranged by intergovernmental organizations.

garrison state   A totalitarian state organized economically and politically as though it were a political organization. Also a nation that is in a state of constant readiness for war.

General Agreement on Tariffs and Trade (GATT)   A multilateral agreement for the promotion of equal treatment for all trading nations, negotiated tariff reductions, and the elimination of import quotas.

General Assembly   The major organ of the United Nations in which all members are equally represented. It is a continuing international conference and an international forum in which each member nation can discuss its international problems with all others.

genocide   The deliberate and concerted attempt on the part of a government to exterminate an entire political or ethnic minority group.

geopolitics   The theory and practice of international politics which emphasizes the importance of the geographical position of political units.

government   Authority exercised through formal or bureaucratic means; the techniques, laws, processes, and agencies through which political officials regulate and maintain order. Also the people in political office, whether elected or appointed, who exercise authority over a citizenry in a political unit.

government-in-exile   A group of governmental personnel who continue to function as a body in another country, although they had been forcibly driven from their own country by an outside invader.

green revolution   The development and widespread adoption of high-yielding strains of wheat, corn, and rice in the Third World. Used especially to describe the increase in agricultural production in India in the 1960s and 1970s, it now refers to almost any program of modern agricultural technology introduced into the Third World.

gross national product   The total value of all final goods and services produced by a nation in a given year.

headlands theory   The view that the boundaries of nations should be drawn as straight lines over bodies of water to connect peninsulas or capes, rather than following the shoreline a few miles out into the body of water.

historicism   The view that social and cultural trends can be described only for specific societies, but not in any meaningful way for human society in general.

holy war   A violent conflict in which the masses of fighters struggle for the preservation or extension of their religious beliefs.

human geography   The study of the spatial distribution of populations, and their use of their natural environments.

ideology   The principles that underlie the structure of a government, economic system, or social movement.

imperialism   The ideology that justifies the acquisition and control of foreign lands in order to exploit their natural resources and bind them economically and politically to the dominant nation.

import-substitution   Government policies to encourage the domestic production of goods that are currently imported, often to improve a country's balance of payments or increase self-sufficiency.

infant mortality rate   The number of deaths among children under age one per thousand live births.

insurgency   In international law, a recognized rebellion or revolution that is not so well organized nor fully recognized to constitute a legal conflict between parties of equal status.

insurrection   A violent uprising by armed and organized opponents to the established political authority in a given state. Insurrectionists are not generally recognized as a government to deal with in international circles because their status is usually uncertain.

intergovernmental organizations (IGOs)   International organizations composed of representatives of national governments in either global or regional groupings for various political and economic reasons.

International Bank for Reconstruction and Development (IBRD)   An agency of the United Nations that was established in 1945 to help finance the reconstruction of postwar Europe and continues to promote the economic development of developing countries.

International Court of Justice (ICJ)   An international tribunal established as one of the six major organs of the United Nations to adjudicate disputes among nations.

international law   A body of rules and principles that guides the relations among nations and between governments and foreign nationals. Sources of international law include treaties, international courts, reason, and custom.

International Monetary Fund (IMF)   Established in 1945 to promote stability in the international monetary system, the IMF is a fund from which member governments can borrow foreign currency to meet balance-of-payments deficits. Loans are granted provided the receiving country adopts a plan to correct the deficit.

internationalism   The theory and practice of national involvement in cooperative interstate efforts to solve common security, political, economic, and social problems.

isolationism   The theory and practice of noninvolvement in affairs of other nations. As a political ideology, isolationism is nurtured by geographical, ideological, and cultural separateness.

jingoism   The endorsement of war as a method of promoting national interest.

joint equity venture   A cooperative arrangement between business firms without legal corporate ties to pursue jointly particular economic activities.

junta   Spanish term for a small group of revolutionaries who seek to capture control of their government by military action.

jurisdiction   The authority assigned to a given court by a legislative body or by a constitution. Also the territory over which authority is exercised.

kakistocracy   Government or domination by the worst elements of society.

land reform   Reorganization of the existing land ownership and management to bring about a more equitable division of agricultural land.

law   All the statutes, treaties, and ordinances that have been passed by legislative bodies.

League of Nations   The first general international organization established to preserve peace and security and to promote cooperation among nations in economic and social fields. The League was formed in 1919 by the victorious powers of World War I under the leadership of U.S. President Woodrow Wilson, but the United States did not join. The League voted itself out of existence in 1946 as a consequence of its failure to prevent World War II. Its assets were transferred to the newly formed United Nations.

less-developed countries   Countries that are also described as "developing."

life expectancy at birth   The number of years an infant born in a particular year can be expected to live, given current conditions of mortality.

literacy rate, adult   The percentage of the population age fifteen and over that can read and write.

Lome Convention   An economic cooperative arrangement between the European community and about 50 African, Caribbean, and Western Pacific developing countries to provide preferential access of imports and exports among member nations, as well as financial aid and technical assistance.

macroeconomics   The study of entire economic systems, as totalities.

market economy   An economic system in which buyers and sellers exchange goods and services on the basis of supply and demand.

martial law   System of maintaining law and order through military force.

mediation   A way of seeking a solution to a dispute, where a third party tries to aid the disputants to reach an agreement.

megalopolis   A large city.

mercantilism   The view that a government of a state should regulate the commercial transactions of its citizens who deal with foreign businessmen so that a surplus of precious metals is accumulated in the native country.

metropolis   A large urban area made up of several constitutent urban communities.

microeconomics   The study of small economic enterprises, or the study of the importance of a given commodity in an economy.

migrant   A person who is changing his/her place of residence, or one who wanders about with no permanent place of residence.

migration   The movement of people from one place to another.

militarism   The belief in and heavy reliance on a military establishment to enforce the foreign policies and further the national interests of a state.

mixed economy   An economic system in which free enterprise is affected by government regulations.

monetary union   The complete harmonization of monetary policies among the countries of a regional economic cooperative arrangement such as the European community, and the eventual emergence of a uniform, transnational currency.

money   Any material thing that is acceptable as a medium of exchange, and which serves as a standard of value. Good money is also portable; relatively durable; uniform in size, shape, and quality; divisible; easily recognizable; difficult to counterfeit; and relatively stable in value.

most-favored-nation status   Participation in a trading system in which all tariff concessions agreed upon by negotiating states are extended to all other states.

multilateral aid   Contributions from several countries to an intermediary institution, such as the World Bank, which then allocates the assistance to the recipient.

national interest   The concept of the security and well-being of the state, used in making foreign policy. The concept holds that security and national advantage are the paramount considerations in state actions.

nationalism   The cohesive element of the nation-state that is the strong identification with and loyalty to that state by the people of that state. This loyalty has as its main elements common values, traditions, historical experiences, language background, and similar ethnic composition.

nationalization   The act of placing an industry or other institutional activity under the ownership and control of a national government.

nation-state   An abstract entity made up of the citizens, territory, and government of a self-identified unit that exists as a sovereign entity under international law.

natural law   A law considered as flowing from morality, natural justice, and the rational nature of humans, as opposed to a law made by legislatures or international treaties.

natural rate of increase of population   The rate at which a population
grows over a given period, due to an excess of births over deaths.
The rate is expressed as a percentage of the base population. It may
be found by subtracting the crude death rate from the crude birth rate.
This measure excludes population changes resulting from immigration
and emigration.

neo-functionalism   A concept that asserts that the forces of functionalism
must receive a special impetus to be effective. Thus regional institutions are
created to further regional integration.

neutralism   A third element in the cold war power struggle composed
of states that pursue policies of nonalignment toward the capitalist and
Communist blocs. Many of the nations of Asia, Africa, and the Middle East
and a few states of Latin America and Europe have refused to join military
alliance systems propagated by either the United States or the Soviet Union.
Political neutralism is not equal to legal neutrality.

neutrality   The legal status of a nation that does not participate in wars
between other states. Under international law, such a state is free to defend
its own territory or neutral waters against attack by belligerents.

New International Economic Order (NIEO)   A set of proposals for
structural change in the international economy that were made by
developing countries in the United Nations and were adopted by the
UN General Assembly in 1974. These proposals are designed to correct
international economic imbalances felt by developing nations.

newly industrializing countries   Countries that have developed effective
strategies for using their resources to advance national industrialization.
These nations include Taiwan, South Korea, and Hong Kong.

nongovernmental organizations (NGOs)   Regional and global groups that
spring from a variety of sources: multinational enterprises (MNEs), religious
denominations, welfare and scientific organizations, cultural and charitable
foundations, transnational political parties, terrorist organizations, and
fraternal orders. These groups are increasingly impacting international
relations.

North Atlantic Treaty Organization (NATO)   An organization established
to create a single unified defense force to safeguard the security of the North
Atlantic area.

North-South dialogue   Talks and negotiations between the economically
advanced countries, mostly located in the Northern Hemisphere, and the
developing countries, mostly located in the Southern Hemisphere, about the
improvement of the economic welfare of the latter and the supply of raw
materials to the former.

oligarchy   Government or domination by a small clique.

oligopoly   The control of a market by a few competing producers or suppliers, each of whom can influence the price of a given commodity to some extent.

operational clause   The acceptance by national governments of the compulsory jurisdiction of the International Court of Justice. Many governments, including the United States, accept this jurisdiction only with considerable reservations.

Organization for Economic Cooperation and Development (OECD)   An organization designed to further economic growth and to contribute to the development of the world economy by encouraging cooperation among its members and promoting technical analysis of economic trends.

Organization of American States (OAS)   A regional political organization, composed of the United States and twenty Latin-American republics, created to institutionalize the principles of the Monroe Doctrine.

pacifism   The political point of view that advocates the maintenance of peaceful conditions even after severe provocation.

patriotism   The advocation and support of the independence and integrity of a national state.

per capita GNP   The gross national product of a nation, divided by its population.

persona non grata   An unacceptable person; especially relating to situations in which a nation declares that an ambassador or minister is no longer acceptable and requests his or her recall.

Physical Quality of Life Index (PQLI)   A composite measure of human well-being that combines the infant mortality rate, life expectancy at age one, and the literacy rate. Individual countries are ranked on a relative scale of 0 (low) to 100 (high).

politics   The exercise of power over others. Also the methods intended to influence the decisions and actions of others. The authoritative allocation of values.

population age structure   The composition, by age, of a given population, expressed as a percentage of the population for each age category. The population age/sex structure is the percentage of population of each sex in different age categories.

population growth rate   The rate at which a population grows in a given year. Includes increases resulting from immigration and emigration.

population pyramid   A graph showing the composition of a population with reference to age and sex.

positive law   A term that refers to the laws that are enacted by a government of men as distinct from the concepts of divine law or natural law.

private voluntary organization   A nongovernmental, not-for-profit organization.

progress   Social or cultural change in the direction of a certain goal.

proliferation, nuclear   The spread of nuclear weapons.

protectionism   The view that the tariff laws of a country should be designed to protect home industries against foreign competition.

protectorate   A political unit that has international recognition as a unique political entity, but whose foreign relations are controlled by another nation.

protocol   The proper ceremonial language and the recognition of status among diplomats.

puppet state   A state whose policies are controlled by another state.

quid pro quo   A diplomatic bargaining concept meaning, literally, "something for something."

rapprochement   The reestablishment of friendly diplomatic relations between two governments.

rational policy model   The notion that the making of foreign policy is done through a rational intellectual process.

realpolitik   Practical politics; power politics.

recognition   The discretionary function exercised by the government for deciding whether or not the nation shall officially carry on relations with a new state or a new political regime in an existing state.

refugee   A person who is driven out of a country by the government of his/her homeland and must take refuge in another nation to avoid persecution.

representative government   The form of government in which power is exercised by the freely elected representatives of a citizenry.

republic   A government by the freely elected representatives of the people.

revolution   A relatively sudden and comprehensive change in the basic practices and ideas in a society.

Roman law   As a source for international law, this concept stems from laws of the Roman Empire, which were seen as the sum of principles that control human conduct.

sanctions   A collective punitive action involving diplomatic, economic, or military measures against a state.

Second World   Nations of the Communist world, with controlled economies.

Secretariat   An organized body of officials and civil servants who maintain the administrative functions of the United Nations.

secretary-general   The chief administrative officer of the United Nations. The secretary-general is chosen by the General Assembly, upon recommendation by the Security Council, for a five-year term.

Security Council   The organ of the United Nations given primary responsibility for maintaining peace and security in the world. The five permanent members of the Council are Britain, China, France, the Soviet Union, and the United States. They are joined by ten nonpermanent members elected by the General Assembly for two-year periods. A negative vote cast by any permanent member constitutes a veto and stops all action.

self-government   The exercise of government powers by a population in its own interest.

separatism   The political point of view on the part of the members of a given nationality in a multinational state to secede and form their own independent nation.

Social Darwinism   The view that cultural groups and races are subject to the same laws of natural selection as plants and animals in nature. Thus, the weak groups are eventually eliminated, whereas the strong groups grow in numbers as well as in their cultural influence over the weak.

socialism   Any of the idea systems that advocate the collective ownership of property and natural resources.

socialization   The learning process through which people acquire political orientations and patterns of behavior.

sovereignty   That power in a state whose actions are not subject to the control of any other human will.

standard of living   An ideal or expressed level of living.

state socialism   A system of political and economic organization in which the government owns and controls all the means of production and distribution.

statism   A system that favors the total concentration of political power in a central government.

strategic   In the military sense, describes weapons or forces capable of directly affecting another nation's war-making ability.

subsistence farming   A farming enterprise that produces just enough to meet the barest needs of the farm operator.

subversion   Any act that would aid in the overthrow of the government by illegal methods and subordinate it to domination by another state.

supranational power   The authority of intergovernmental organizations to exercise certain powers transferred to them by sovereign states and normally only exercised by the latter.

tactics   Battlefield operations of a local, limited scale.

tariff   A tax charged on the shipment of goods across national borders.

tax   Compulsory payments to a government for the purpose of supporting its activities and functions.

technocracy   A proposed form of government and system of economy in which the major decision-making powers would be the responsibility of engineers and technicians.

technology   The body of knowledge and techniques that pertain to the production of goods.

temporal power   The political power that is based on the allegiance of a citizenry to a state, as distinguished from ecclesiastical authority.

territoriality   The tendency of governments and institutions to protect certain people, land, space, and objects as their own against invasion by others.

terrorism   The technique of public control by impressing the people with ruthless, violent, painful measures as a means of punishment for opposition.

theocracy   Government or domination by clergy acting as the agents of God.

Third World   Non-Communist nations that are relatively poor, but are developing their resources.

totalitarianism   Ideas and practices that seek to implement the concentration of absolute political power in a central government.

transnational relations   Interactions and relations between nongovernmental groups and individuals of different countries as well as between these actors, governments, and intergovernmental organizations across national boundaries.

treaty   A formal agreement entered into between two or more countries. The treaty process includes negotiation, signing, ratification, exchange of ratifications, publishing and proclamation, and treaty execution. Multinational treaties have become the major source of international law.

Trusteeship Council   One of six major organs of the United Nations, established to help the General Assembly supervise the administration of the international trusteeship system. Trust territories include former mandates of the League of Nations, Axis colonies, and colonies voluntarily placed under trusteeship.

tyranny   The arbitrary use of political power.

ultimatum   The final attempt at negotiation on a particular issue before drastic action is taken.

United Nations International Children's Fund (UNICEF)   A UN organization designed to integrate health, water supply, education, nutrition, and emergency famine relief to solve the problems of the most disadvantaged children of the world.

universal cultural pattern   Cultural elements, social organizations, and types of social conduct that can be found in every human society.

universals   Rules of social conduct that are binding on all the people in a given society.

utopia   A proposed ideal society in which people would be happy because all of their problems would be solved.

value   Any object, situation, ideal, principle, or norm that a person or a group of people consider desirable and worthy.

veto   An executive disapproval of a legislative bill or joint resolution.

vital statistics   The raw figures on births, deaths, and marriages in a given population.

war   An organized, sustained, and planned violent conflict between large aggregates of people that is directed by specialists in warfare. War is carried on in the name of a state or society of people rather than for personal reasons of the combatants.

Warsaw Treaty Organization (Warsaw Pact)   A mutual security alliance established in 1955 among Bulgaria, Czechoslovakia,

East Germany, Hungary, Poland, Romania, and the Union of Soviet Socialist Republics.

wealth   Any valued material thing that has utility and that can be transferred, given, or sold by one person to another. Human capabilities may also be included in the concept, although they are not material.

welfare state   A government that provides services for the individual well-being of the citizenry as well as performing the usual regulatory functions of government.

World Bank   This generic term can refer to the World Bank group—three separately funded but closely related agencies including the International Bank for Reconstruction and Development (IBRD); the International Development Association; and the International Finance Corporation. Sometimes the term refers only to the IBRD.

World Health Organization (WHO)   Established by the United Nations in 1948, WHO plans and coordinates health action on a global basis.

world outlook   The cultural frame of reference, or ethos, of a given society. The manner in which the members mentally organize their social world and try to make sense out of it.

xenocentrism   The frame of reference in which a foreign group is looked upon as the possessor of everything desirable and valuable, while the native group is evaluated in reference to the foreign group.

xenophobia   An exaggerated dislike or aversion for strangers or their ways.

Index

213